The Culinary Institute of America

one dish meals

FLAVORFUL SINGLE-DISH MEALS FROM THE WORLD'S PREMIER CULINARY COLLEGE

Over 150 New Delicious, Kitchen-Tested Recipes • 100 Color Photographs
Illustrated Step-by-step Techniques from the Classrooms of the CIA

Photography by Ben Fink

LEBHAR-FRIEDMAN BOOKS

NEW YORK • CHICAGO • LOS ANGELES • LONDON • PARIS • TOKYO

THE CULINARY INSTITUTE OF AMERICA

President	Dr. Tim Ryan
Vice-President, Continuing Education	Mark Erickson
Director of Intellectual Property	Nathalie Fischer
Managing Editor	Kate McBride
Editorial Project Manager	Mary Donovan
Editorial Assistant	Margaret Otterstrom
Production Assistant	Patrick Decker

*The Culinary Institute of America would like to thank Chef Bruce Mattel for his
skilled execution and presentation of the recipes and methods for the photographs, and Chef Mattel and
his family for inviting us into their home for the photography.*

*Special thanks to Warren Cutlery in Rhinebeck, New York, for providing
some of the items used in the photography.*

LEBHAR-FRIEDMAN BOOKS

A company of Lebhar-Friedman, Inc., 425 Park Avenue, New York, New York 10022

Project Manager	Maria Tufts
Art Director	Kevin Hanek

LIBRARY OF CONGRESS CATALOGING-IN-PUBLICATION DATA

Cataloging-in-publication data for this title is on file with the Library of Congress.

ISBN 0-86730-908-3 | 978-0-86730-908-9

Manufactured in Singapore on acid-free paper

contents

introduction

What is a one dish meal?

YOUR FIRST REACTION to the title of this book may very well be to imagine a large soup pot sitting on a stove and bubbling away. We began thinking about some traditional options: stews, braises, hearty soups, and layered pasta dishes like lasagna.

We also took a look around at what everyone else was saying about one dish meals and we found a lot of different names for this style of cooking:

- *Fix it and forget it*
- *Cook once a week (or once a month)*
- *Meals that make themselves*
- *Slow cooking*
- *Peasant cooking*
- *Wash-day cooking*
- *Sabbath meals*

When you look at the list, you begin to realize that it's all about taking charge of the time you spend in the kitchen. Sabbath meals, for instance, are made the night before and left to cook so that prohibitions against working on the Sabbath can be observed. Wash-day meals are the answer to making dinner on a day when the cook simply can't be spared from other household chores. Peasant cooking is all about coaxing flavor from foods and frugality. Cooking once a week or once a month is a way to avoid the feeling that you cooked all day just to have your work devoured in ten minutes.

The more we thought about it, the more we realized that you can make a one dish meal without using any pots and pans at all. What is a sandwich or a pizza but a one dish meal? Then we thought about dishes like chef's salad, delicate omelets, silken quiches, and tender-crisp stir-fries. We realized that we needed to define what we mean by a one dish meal carefully, because we didn't want to leave anything out.

Cooks have more than one need and a more complex culinary personality than some books give them credit for. This book accommodates a trusty pot roast that you leave alone in a gentle oven as well as a fiery curry from Thailand that cooks in less time than the nightly news. You'll find dishes that cook for hours and dishes that are not "cooked" at all but are simply built, composed, or assembled. As we worked on this book, we smashed some one dish "myths."

Myth #1: One dish meals are only for cold weather.

One dish meals can be served anytime of the year, in any kind of weather. Some are rib-sticking classics like cassoulet or pot roasts that do call out for a nip in the air and a fire in the grate. Others are perfect for the dog days of summer.

Myth #2: One dish meals take hours and hours to cook.

Yes, stews and braises can take hours to cook. Dishes based on beans take a long time, too, but you can put together a one-dish, main-course salad or sandwich in about 15 minutes. If you are making a stir-fried or sautéed dish, you may have a bit of prep to do beforehand, but once you start to cook you are finished in a short time, often less than 10 minutes.

Myth #3: One dish meals are comforting, but staid.

You can't deny the magic of a melt-in-your-mouth stew, and we've made sure that those dishes are represented here. That said, we know that building flavor into every dish is one way to make sure that your stews stand out. Whether you are using culinary techniques to build flavor (sautéing onions

for aroma, for instance) or introducing pungent ingredients like capers, anchovies, or lemongrass, you can count on rich, fully-developed flavors.

Preparing a One Dish Meal

There are three basic approaches to preparing a one dish meal. Some dishes may straddle the line between categories, but just as a basic guide:

PUT IT IN THE POT OR PAN, LET IT COOK, THEN SERVE This category includes soups, stews, braises, stir-fries, sautés, and omelets. These are generally the dishes that require the most "cooking," in the sense that they will require your attention at the stove for their preparation.

ASSEMBLE THEN SERVE This category includes dishes like sandwiches and salads. The real effort in preparing most of these kinds of dishes is the ingredient preparation. However, some ingredients can be obtained already prepared, making assembling the dish even easier.

ASSEMBLE IN A POT OR PAN, LET IT COOK "ON ITS OWN," THEN SERVE This category includes pasta dishes, casseroles and gratins, and pizza. These dishes can be prepared with a minimum of time spent in the kitchen during the actual cooking, which can take place unattended for a long stretch of time before needing to be dealt with further.

As you can see, a variety of dishes, food types, and preparation techniques can be thought of in terms of their "one dish" adaptability. The consisistent theme among them all seems to be an emphasis on concise preparation and serving, as well as a focus on a few simple ingredients or meal components.

We hope that you enjoy the collection of one dish meals in this book, and that it will become the inspiration for dinner, whether you are cooking *en famille* or for a friendly gathering.

soups

WE LOOK TO soup as nourishment, comfort, and ease. When we decide to serve a soup, we should consider a couple things. What is the season? What vegetables are at their peak? A brimming bowl of Gazpacho is wonderful in the late summer when tomatoes are at their peak. A hearty Senate Bean Soup is perfect for winter's dark nights.

For many cooks, a pot of soup simmering on the stove is more than a frugal way to wring the last bit of nourishment and flavor from foods. There are a number of soups that can easily accommodate a little bit of this or a few spoonfuls of that. However, soup should not be used to try and disguise leftovers that are past their prime. Remember that the soup you produce will only be as good as what went into it.

Most soup recipes are exceptionally forgiving and can easily adapt to meet the needs of the moment. Feel free to improvise with ingredients. A broth-based soup with lots of fresh vegetables can usually accommodate a few beans or lentils to make a rib-sticking winter meal. You can double or even triple most recipes to prepare batches to eat now and freeze for later. You can even decide to serve a soup chilled instead of hot.

However, while simmering most soups for 10 or 15 minutes longer than the recommended cooking time won't normally make a big difference, it is important to know that soups can be overcooked. When a soup is cooked too long, it becomes flat and tasteless. Pureed soups, or those with ingredients like beans and potatoes, can scorch easily. The way to check your soup is to taste it from time to time as it simmers. Stop cooking just as soon as you like the way it tastes and all the ingredients are properly tender.

The soup recipes in this chapter encompass a wide variety of soup styles. Some are thick and creamy, others are rich broths garnished with plenty of fresh vegetables and herbs. The key to success with any of these recipes is the quality of the ingredients you choose.

One of the most important of all ingredients is the liquid the soup is "built" upon. A richly flavored broth is at the heart of many of these soups. You can make your own but even the chefs who teach at the CIA don't shy away from buying broths at the store. They do have a few words of advice: Look for good quality ingredients including good cuts of meats, fish or poultry, and fresh vegetables and herbs. Opt for low- or reduced-sodium brands if they are available. Resealable packaging makes it easy to keep broth on hand and convenient to use. If you are choosing a soup base rather than a broth, check the label carefully and be sure to follow the instructions for diluting the base. You may want to add two or three sprigs of parsley or other fresh herbs as the soup simmers for a fresher, brighter flavor.

fisherman's soup with shrimp and fresh herbs

Canh Chua Tom

i T IS worth the effort to find a fresh pineapple for this soup. You may be able to find peeled and cored fresh pineapple in the produce section of your grocery store.

SERVES 6

2 tbsp peanut oil

2 tbsp Vietnamese chili paste

2 tsp minced garlic

10 cups chicken broth

2 cups quartered cherry tomatoes

1 cup diced pineapple

¼ cup tamarind pulp

2 tbsp Vietnamese fish sauce, plus as needed

1 tbsp sugar

1 lb shrimp (31-35 count), peeled, deveined, halved lengthwise

½ cup diced taro root

2 tbsp lime juice, or as needed

Salt as needed

Freshly ground black pepper as needed

¾ cup bean sprouts, trimmed

¼ cup cilantro leaves

6 Thai basil leaves, cut in halves

Crispy fried shallots (see page 11)

1. Heat the oil in a soup pot over medium heat. Add the chili paste and garlic, and sauté until fragrant, stirring constantly, about 20 seconds. Add the chicken broth, tomatoes, pineapple, tamarind, 2 tablespoons of the fish sauce, and the sugar. Bring the broth to a boil, stirring to dissolve the tamarind paste.

2. As soon as the soup comes to a boil, reduce the heat and simmer until flavorful, about 5 minutes. Add the shrimp and taro root, and simmer just until the shrimp is barely cooked through, 5 minutes.

3. Season the soup to taste with the lime juice, additional fish sauce, salt, and pepper. Divide the shrimp, bean sprouts, cilantro, and basil equally among 6 warmed soup bowls. Ladle the warm broth over the shrimp and garnishes, top with the fried shallots, and serve at once.

CLOCKWISE FROM UPPER LEFT *When frying shallots, pull them out of the oil just before they're finished because they will continue to cook for a short time after being removed from the heat. Taro root, also called dasheen in the southern United States, can be found in ethnic markets or specialty produce stores. Tamarind is the fruit of a tall shade tree indigenous to Asia and northern Africa and is available in many Indian and Asian markets as a concentrated pulp, canned paste or whole "brick" of dried pods. When preparing this soup, keep the prepared broth warm as you fill the bowls with garnish, then ladle the warm broth into the bowl just before serving.*

portuguese potato kale soup

Caldo Verde

CALDO VERDE, literally "green soup," is a robust, incredibly satisfying concoction of kale, garlic, and smoky meats in a silky pureed potato soup base. Linguiça, a Portuguese garlic sausage, can be found in many supermarkets and Latin American markets. If you can't locate it, try substituting smoked kielbasa.

MAKES 8 SERVINGS

1 tbsp olive oil

¾ cup diced leek, white and light green part

¾ cup diced onion

¼ cup diced celery

5 cups chicken broth

4 russet potatoes, peeled, cut into sixths

1 smoked ham hock

1½ cups chopped kale

2 oz linguiça sausage, diced (about ½ link)

½ bay leaf

Salt as needed

Freshly ground black pepper as needed

1. Heat the oil in a soup pot over medium heat. Add the leek, onion, and celery. Cook, stirring occasionally, until the onion is translucent, 4 to 6 minutes.

2. Add the broth, potatoes, and ham hock. Bring to a simmer and cook until the meat and vegetables are very tender, about 40 minutes.

3. Meanwhile, bring a large pot of salted water to a rolling boil. Use a paring knife to cut away the tough stems from the kale and discard them. Blanch the kale in the boiling water until it wilts, about 3 minutes. Drain the kale, run it under cold water to stop the cooking, and drain again. Slice the kale into thin shreds.

4. Remove the ham hock from the soup base and set aside. Puree the soup base, return it to the pot, and bring to a simmer.

5. When the ham hock is cool enough to handle, remove the meat from the bone and cut into small dice. Add the diced ham, kale, sausage, and bay leaf to the soup base. Season to taste with salt and pepper and simmer 15 to 20 minutes longer. Serve in heated bowls.

borscht

borscht is one of those soups that has dozens of variations. This version of the classic Russian beet soup uses lots of vegetables and a touch of bacon for extra flavor. You can leave out the bacon and use vegetable broth if you prefer a vegetarian soup. Grating the beets into the soup releases maximum beet flavor and color.

MAKES 8 SERVINGS

2 medium beets

2 tbsp minced bacon

2½ cups minced onion

1 cup celery matchsticks

⅔ cup parsnip matchsticks

⅓ cup carrot matchsticks

1¼ cups leek matchsticks, white and light green parts

2 cups shredded Savoy cabbage

8 cups chicken or vegetable broth, plus as needed

Sachet: 1 tsp dried marjoram, 4 to 5 parsley stems, 2 cloves peeled garlic, and 1 bay leaf enclosed in a large tea ball or tied in a cheesecloth pouch

Red wine vinegar as needed

Salt as needed

Freshly ground black pepper as needed

½ cup sour cream

¼ cup minced dill

1. Simmer the beets in enough boiling water to cover until partially cooked, 10 to 15 minutes. When cool enough to handle, peel and reserve for later. (Use gloves to keep your hands from turning purple.)

2. Cook the bacon in a soup pot over medium heat until crisp, 6 to 8 minutes.

3. Add the onion, celery, parsnip, carrot, leek, and cabbage. Cover and cook over low heat, stirring occasionally, until the vegetables are translucent, about 15 minutes.

4. Add the broth and sachet. Bring to a simmer and cook for 10 minutes.

5. Grate the parboiled beets (wear gloves) directly into the soup and simmer until all the vegetables are tender, about 10 minutes.

6. Remove and discard the sachet. Season to taste with the vinegar, salt, and pepper. Serve in heated bowls, garnished with the sour cream and dill.

PHEASANT BORSCHT

Remove the neck and giblets from the cavity of a 2½-pound pheasant. Rinse the cavity with cold water and place the pheasant in a soup pot. Add the 8 cups of chicken broth from above plus more as needed to cover the pheasant. Bring to a simmer over low heat and cook, skimming as needed, until the pheasant meat is tender, about 45 minutes. Remove the pheasant from the broth and cool. Strain the broth through a fine sieve lined with cheesecloth. When the pheasant is cool enough to handle, skin it and remove the meat from the carcass. Discard the skin and bones and shred the meat. Use 8 cups of the pheasant broth instead of the chicken broth. Add the shredded pheasant meat to the soup just before seasoning it.

udon noodle pot

UDON NOODLES are sold as both a fresh and dry pasta. We used fresh noodles in this recipe, but you can substitute dried udon noodles. To learn about preparing them, see the note below.

MAKES 6 SERVINGS

24 oz fresh udon noodles

1 tbsp peanut or canola oil

6 cups dashi (recipe follows)

2 dozen littleneck clams

12 oz boneless skinless chicken thighs, cut into bite-size pieces

12 oz small shrimp (31–36 count), peeled and deveined

1½ cups sliced shiitake mushroom caps

1½ cups finely shredded Napa cabbage

1½ cups finely shredded spinach

1 cup thinly sliced carrots

1 cup snow peas, trimmed

⅓ cup soy sauce

1 tbsp mirin

2 scallions, thinly sliced on the diagonal

1. Bring a large pot of salted water to a boil. Cook the noodles until just tender, about 2 to 3 minutes. Drain the noodles and rinse under cold water. Drain the noodles again, toss with the oil, and reserve.

2. Bring the dashi to a simmer in the pot. Add the clams, chicken, shrimp, and mushrooms to the pot and ladle the simmering dashi over the top. Cover the pot and cook until the clams are open and the chicken is cooked through, 10 to 12 minutes. Discard any clams that do not open. Transfer the clams, shrimp, chicken, and mushrooms to a bowl and keep warm.

3. Add the cabbage, spinach, carrots, and snow peas to the pot and simmer until all of the vegetables are cooked through and very hot, about 10 minutes. Return the noodles to the pot and simmer until they are very hot, 3 to 4 minutes. Add the soy sauce and mirin and continue to simmer until the soup is very flavorful, 2 to 3 minutes.

4. Serve the clams, chicken, shrimp, and mushrooms over the noodles and vegetables and ladle the broth over the top. Garnish with the scallions.

Dashi

MAKES 6 CUPS

6½ cups cold water

One 3-inch piece dried kombu seaweed

2 oz bonito flakes

Combine the water, kombu, and bonito flakes in a large saucepan. Bring the water to a simmer over medium-high heat. Continue to simmer until the broth is very flavorful, 20 to 25 minutes. Strain the broth and use as directed. (Dashi can be stored in a clean covered container in the refrigerator for up to 1 week.)

PREPARING UDON NOODLES

To prepare fresh udon noodles: bring a large pot of salted water to a rolling boil over high heat. Add the noodles, stir to separate the strands, and cook until they are tender to the bite, but not mushy, 2 to 4 minutes.

To prepare dried udon noodles, begin as you do for fresh noodles by bringing water to a rolling boil and adding the noodles. Then, once the water returns to a boil, add 1 cup of cold water. Repeat the process of bringing the water back to a boil and adding a cup of cold water two or three more times or until the noodles are tender.

cioppino

a SAVORY TOMATO broth full of seafood and vegetables, cioppino is an American original created in San Francisco by Italian immigrants. It's a meal in and of itself. Although not traditional, you can substitute 1 cup of lump crab meat for the crabs. If you purchase fennel with the tops still attached, save some of the nicest looking sprigs for a garnish. Serve the cioppino with large garlic toasts or crusty sourdough bread.

MAKES 8 TO 10 SERVINGS

2 tbsp olive oil

1½ cups sliced scallions

2 cups diced green pepper

1¼ cups diced onion

1¼ cups diced fennel bulb

2 tsp minced garlic

1 cup dry white wine

4 cups fish broth

8 cups chopped plum tomatoes, fresh or canned

½ cup tomato puree

2 bay leaves

Salt as needed

Freshly ground black pepper as needed

20 littleneck clams, scrubbed well

3 steamed hard-shell crabs, cooked

20 medium shrimp, peeled and deveined

1¼ lb swordfish or halibut steaks, diced

3 tbsp minced basil

1. Heat the oil in a soup pot over medium heat. Add the scallions, pepper, onion, and fennel. Cook, stirring occasionally, until the onion is translucent, 6 to 8 minutes. Add the garlic and cook another minute. Add the white wine, bring to a boil, and cook until the volume of wine is reduced by about half, 4 to 6 minutes.

2. Add the fish broth, tomatoes, tomato puree, and bay leaves. Cover and slowly simmer the mixture for about 45 minutes. Add a small amount of water, if necessary. Cioppino should be more a broth than a stew.

3. Season to taste with the salt and pepper. Remove and discard the bay leaves. Add the clams and simmer for about 10 minutes. Discard any clams that do not open.

4. Separate the claws from the crabs and cut the bodies in half. Add the crab pieces, shrimp, and swordfish to the soup. Simmer until the fish is just cooked through, about 5 minutes.

5. Add the basil and adjust the seasoning to taste, if necessary. Serve in heated bowls or soup plates.

chicken vegetable soup azteca

ONCE AN important food for the Aztec and Maya peoples of Central America, the chayote is a pear-shaped fruit with furrowed, pale green skin. It is also known variously as a mirliton, a christophene, and a vegetable pear. It has a rather mild flavor that has been described as a blend of cucumber, zucchini, and kohlrabi.

MAKES 8 SERVINGS

1 chayote

3 tbsp olive oil

1 poblano chile

1 tsp minced garlic

2 tbsp minced jalapeño pepper

1 tsp ground coriander

1½ lb boneless, skinless chicken breasts, diced

6 cups chicken broth

5 canned Italian plum tomatoes, chopped

1 cup diced onion

⅓ cup diced carrot

½ cup diced celery

1 cup diced yellow squash

1 tbsp chopped cilantro

Salt as needed

Freshly ground black pepper as needed

1. Preheat the oven to 350°F. Rub the chayote with 1 teaspoon of the oil and place it on a baking sheet. Roast the chayote in the oven until the skin browns lightly and the flesh becomes barely tender, 25 to 30 minutes. When cool enough to handle, use a paring knife to scrape away the skin. Cut the chayote in half from top to bottom and use a spoon to scoop out the edible seed, which you can either discard or eat as a snack. Dice the flesh and set aside.

2. Increase the oven temperature to broil. Brush the poblano with 1 teaspoon of the oil. Place it under the broiler and turn it as it roasts so that it blackens evenly on all sides. Transfer the poblano to a small bowl and cover tightly. Let it steam for 10 minutes, then remove it from the bowl and pull off the skin. Use the back of a knife to scrape away any bits that don't come away easily. Remove and discard the seeds, ribs, and stem. Dice the flesh and set aside.

3. Heat the remaining oil in a soup pot over medium heat. Add the garlic, jalapeño pepper, and coriander. Cook, stirring occasionally, until slightly softened, about 4 minutes. Add the chicken and cook, stirring occasionally, until the chicken is just cooked through, about 8 minutes. Add the chayote, poblano, broth, tomatoes, onion, carrot, celery, and yellow squash. Bring to a simmer and cook until all the vegetables are tender, about 30 minutes.

4. Add the cilantro and season to taste with salt and pepper. Serve in heated bowls.

indonesian chicken, noodle, and potato soup

Soto Ayam

dON'T LET the long list of ingredients and steps deter you from making this soup. It's truly delicious and not all that much trouble to make, despite appearances. Any of the ingredients you can't find at your supermarket are available at Asian groceries. To crush the aromatic ingredients, cover them with a piece of plastic wrap and smash with the bottom of a heavy pot or skillet.

MAKES 8 SERVINGS

One 3-lb chicken

2 tsp salt

1 tbsp vegetable oil

4 shallots, chopped

2 stalks fresh lemongrass, bottom 4 or 5 inches only, crushed

1 garlic clove, crushed

One 1-inch slice fresh ginger, crushed

½ tsp crushed black peppercorns

¼ tsp turmeric

6 cups chicken broth

1¼ cups diced yellow or white potatoes

1 oz dried mung bean threads (cellophane noodles)

2 tbsp soy sauce

1 tbsp red chili or hot bean paste

½ tsp sugar

4 scallions, thinly sliced

2 hard-boiled eggs, chopped

½ cup diced celery

1 tsp lemon juice or as needed

Crispy fried shallots for garnish (see note below)

1 lemon, cut into wedges for garnish

1. Remove the giblets from the chicken; discard or save the liver for another use. Wash the chicken and rub it with ½ teaspoon of the salt. Set aside.

2. Heat the oil in a skillet over high heat. Add the chopped shallots, lemongrass, garlic, ginger, black peppercorns, and turmeric. Cook, stirring constantly, until the aroma is apparent, about 30 seconds. Remove the skillet from the heat.

3. Combine the broth and remaining 1½ teaspoons salt with the chicken, giblets, and shallot mixture in a soup pot. Bring to a simmer and cook, skimming often to remove any foam that rises to the surface, until the chicken is cooked through and tender, about 45 minutes. *(continues on page 12)*

CRISPY FRIED SHALLOTS

Some Indonesian dishes are garnished with crispy fried shallots. Select large, firm shallots with smooth skins. Use a sharp paring knife to trim away the ends and pull off the skin. Cut the shallot into thin slices and separate them into rings. Plan on about 1 cup of sliced shallots to make enough garnish for 6 servings. That works out to about 3 large shallots.

Pour an inch of oil (canola, peanut, or olive oils are all suitable) into a small, heavy-gauge saucepan. When it reaches 350 degrees F, add the shallots and fry, stirring them occasionally, until they have a rich, sweet aroma and a good brown color, about 5 minutes.

Use a slotted spoon to lift the fried shallots from the oil. Transfer them to a plate or bowl lined with paper toweling. You can hold them at room temperature for up to one hour.

4. Remove the chicken from the broth and set aside. When cool enough to handle, remove the bones from the chicken. Return the bones to the broth and continue to simmer, skimming as needed, about 1 hour. Meanwhile, dice the chicken meat and set aside.

5. Place the potatoes in a saucepan, cover with cold water, and bring to a simmer. Cook until tender, about 20 minutes. Drain and spread the potatoes in a single layer to cool.

6. Soak the bean threads in hot water to cover until tender, about 5 minutes. Rinse and separate the strands under cool running water. Chop them into 2-inch pieces and set aside.

7. When the broth has simmered for an hour, strain it through a fine sieve, and return it to the pot. Mix the soy sauce, chili paste, and sugar together; stir into the strained broth. Add the diced chicken meat, cooked potatoes, soaked bean threads, scallions, chopped eggs, and celery to the broth. Bring to a simmer and add a squeeze of lemon to taste.

8. Serve the soup in heated bowls, garnished with the fried shallots. Pass the lemon wedges on the side.

callaloo

CALLALOO IS the name for the greens of the taro root. They are popular in the Caribbean, where they are cooked and served in much the same way as collard or turnip greens are in the southeastern United States. Callaloo can be purchased at Caribbean markets, but if you cannot find them in your area, fresh spinach makes a fine substitute. Whichever greens you use, be sure to wash them thoroughly to remove any grit.

MAKES 8 SERVINGS

5 oz slab bacon, rind removed, cut into small dice

¾ cup minced onion

1 tsp minced garlic

8 cups chicken broth

4 cups sliced okra

1½ cups coarsely chopped callaloo (taro greens)

1 Scotch bonnet chile, pricked with a fork and left whole

4 tsp chopped thyme leaves or 2 tsp dried

Salt as needed

Freshly ground black pepper as needed

10 oz crabmeat, picked over for shells

3 scallions, sliced

¾ cup coconut milk

Juice of 2 limes, or more as needed

1. Cook the bacon in a soup pot over medium heat until crisp, about 8 minutes. Add the onion and garlic and cook, stirring occasionally, until softened, about 3 minutes.

2. Add the broth, okra, greens, chile, and thyme along with a pinch of salt and pepper. Bring to a simmer and cook for 30 minutes.

3. Just before serving, remove the chile and add the crabmeat, scallions, coconut milk, and lime juice. Season to taste with salt and pepper. Serve in heated bowls.

hot and sour soup

t HIS CHINESE-STYLE hot and sour soup gets "hot" from white and black peppercorns and "sour" from two kinds of vinegar. With little flavor of their own, dried cloud ears (also known as black fungus, wood ears, or tree ears) soak up the other flavors of the soup and provide a soft, slightly rubbery textural element to this soup. Dried tiger lily buds, also known as golden needles, add texture as well as a slightly sweet or musky flavor.

MAKES 10 TO 12 SERVINGS

2 tbsp dried cloud ears

2 tbsp dried tiger lily buds

1 tbsp vegetable oil

1 tbsp chopped scallion greens

¾ tsp minced ginger root

¼ lb pork butt, ground or cut into matchsticks

1½ cups shredded Napa cabbage

¼ cup drained canned bamboo shoots, thinly sliced

5 cups chicken broth

1 cup diced soft tofu

1 tbsp Chinese black soy sauce

1 tbsp white vinegar

1 tbsp rice vinegar

1 tsp salt, or as needed

¾ tsp freshly ground white pepper

¾ tsp freshly ground black pepper

¼ cup cornstarch dissolved in 2 tbsp cold water

1 egg, lightly beaten

1½ tsp dark (Asian) sesame oil

⅓ cup chopped cilantro

1. Soak the cloud ears and lily buds in enough warm water to cover until softened, about 10 minutes. Drain and rinse well. Cut the stems off the cloud ears and lily buds. Cut the cloud ears in small pieces and the lily buds in half. Set aside.

2. Heat the oil in a large wok or soup pot over medium-high heat. Add the scallion greens and ginger. Stir-fry briefly, about 30 seconds. Add the pork and stir-fry until cooked through, 1 to 2 minutes. Add the cloud ears, lily buds, cabbage, and bamboo shoots. Stir-fry until the cabbage is tender, about 2 minutes.

3. Add the broth and tofu and bring to a simmer. Add the soy sauce, white vinegar, rice vinegar, salt, white pepper, and black pepper.

4. Stir the cornstarch mixture to recombine any starch that has settled to the bottom. While stirring the soup, add about ½ of the cornstarch mixture to the soup. Continue to stir until the soup comes back to a simmer and thickens. The soup should have a slightly thick consistency. If needed, add the remaining cornstarch mixture in small increments to the soup while stirring. Let the soup return to a simmer each time before adding more cornstarch. (Depending on how thick you like your soup, you may not need to use all of the cornstarch.)

5. Stir the egg and sesame oil into the soup and return to a simmer. Serve in heated bowls, garnished with the cilantro.

curried eggplant and lentil soup

*i*N INDIA, where the exact ingredients used in a curry vary from region to region and even from cook to cook, it is usually ground fresh daily. Cooking curry powder in fat before introducing liquid, as is done here, allows the fat to "open up" the fat-soluble flavor compounds in the curry powder for a more flavorful soup.

MAKES 8 SERVINGS

8 cups chicken or vegetable broth

1 cup green or yellow lentils

4 waxy yellow potatoes, such as Yukon Gold or Yellow Finn

1 cup heavy cream

Salt as needed

Freshly ground black pepper as needed

3 tbsp olive oil

2 medium eggplants (about 1 lb each), peeled and diced

1¼ cups finely diced onion

½ tsp minced garlic

2 tbsp curry powder, or as needed

¼ cup fresh lemon juice

¼ cup chopped parsley

1. Simmer the broth, lentils, and potatoes in a soup pot until tender, about 45 minutes.

2. Strain the soup, reserving the liquid. Purée the solids and return the puree to the soup pot. Add the cream and enough of the reserved liquid to achieve a thick soup consistency. Blend well. Season to taste with the salt and pepper. Keep warm.

3. Heat the oil in a skillet over medium heat. Add the eggplant, onion, and garlic; cook for 5 minutes, stirring occasionally. Stir in the curry powder and cook 1 minute more. Add the lemon juice and simmer gently until the eggplant is tender and the lemon juice has evaporated, 2 to 3 minutes. Season to taste with salt and pepper.

4. Add the eggplant mixture to the soup and simmer for 5 to 10 minutes to blend the flavors. Stir in the parsley and serve in heated bowls.

corn and squash soup

THIS SIMPLE soup, based on a freshly made garlic and basil broth, is a wonderful way to take advantage of fresh summer produce. If you crave a taste of summer in the middle of winter, you can also make this soup with frozen corn.

MAKES 4 TO 6 SERVINGS

6 cups water

3 basil sprigs

1 garlic head, halved horizontally

2 tbsp butter

1 cup diced onion

2 cups diced yellow squash

3 cups fresh corn kernels

Salt as needed

Freshly ground black pepper as needed

1. Combine the water, basil, and garlic in a large saucepan. Bring to a simmer and cook, partially covered, for 30 minutes, skimming the surface as necessary. Strain the broth and reserve.

2. Heat the butter in a soup pot over medium heat. Add the onion and cook, stirring frequently, until translucent, about 5 minutes. Add the squash and cook, stirring frequently, for another 5 minutes. Add the corn and reserved broth and bring the soup to a simmer. Season to taste with salt and pepper.

3. Puree the soup and strain it through a fine sieve. Return the soup to the pot and bring to a simmer. Season to taste with salt and pepper. Serve the soup in heated soup bowls.

fresh corn chowder
with Green Chiles and Monterey Jack

THIS CHOWDER is best made with fresh corn on the cob, since you can only get corn milk from the whole ear. After you cut the kernels away, hold the cob over a bowl and use the spine of your knife to scrape out the flavorful juices. Add this corn milk along with the cream when you puree the kernels.

SERVES 8

6 ears of corn, shucked

1 cup heavy cream

2 slices bacon, minced

1¼ cups minced onion

1 cup minced red bell pepper

½ cup minced celery

½ tsp minced garlic clove

6 cups chicken broth

3 cups diced yellow or white potatoes

3 cups chopped tomatoes, peeled and seeded

One 4-oz can green chiles, drained and chopped

1 cup grated Monterey Jack cheese

Salt as needed

Freshly ground black pepper as needed

Tabasco sauce as needed

1 cup corn tortilla strips, toasted, optional

2 tbsp chopped cilantro

1. Cut the corn kernels from the cobs with a sharp knife, capturing as much of the juice as possible. Reserve ¾ cup of the corn kernels for later use. Puree the remaining corn kernels with the heavy cream in a food processor or blender; set aside.

2. Cook the bacon in a soup pot over medium heat until crisp, about 8 minutes. Add the onion, pepper, celery, and garlic. Reduce the heat to low and cover.

3. Cook, stirring occasionally, until the vegetables are tender, 10 to 12 minutes. Add the broth, potatoes, and tomatoes. Bring to a simmer and cook, covered, until the potatoes are tender, about 20 minutes. Skim any fat from the surface and discard.

4. Add the pureed corn and cream, the reserved corn kernels, chiles, and cheese. Cook on low heat just until the corn is warmed, about 5 minutes. Season to taste with salt, pepper, and Tabasco. Serve in heated bowls, garnished with tortilla strips and cilantro.

SMOKED CORN AND POBLANO CHOWDER

CAUTION! Do not try this smoking process unless you have a well-ventilated kitchen. Turn the exhaust fan on high, and monitor the process constantly.

Substitute 2 fresh poblano chiles for the canned green chiles. Core and remove the seeds from the poblanos and the red bell pepper. Cut them into large flat pieces, approximately 4-inches square.

To smoke the corn and peppers, place fine wood chips in a disposable aluminum roasting pan fitted with a wire rack. (If your rack does not have feet, use balls of aluminum foil to raise the rack a few inches above the wood chips.) Use only wood chips that are specifically meant for smoking food. Have ready a fitted cover or sheet of aluminum foil large enough to cover the pan. Heat the roasting pan over high heat until the wood chips begin to smolder and smoke.

Place the corn and pepper sections on the wire rack over the smoking chips. If the chips are smoldering and creating sufficient smoke, remove the pan from the heat. Otherwise, reduce the heat to low. The idea is to keep the chips smoldering, but not to catch them on fire. Cover tightly with the lid or aluminum foil and allow the vegetables to smoke for about 15 to 20 minutes. Remove the cover and allow the vegetables to cool. Dice the red pepper and poblano chile. Follow the recipe above, adding the poblanos at the same time as the red pepper.

fennel and potato chowder

ENNEL, WHICH is sometimes labeled as anise in super-markets, is a vegetable with a broad, bulbous base that can be eaten raw or cooked. It has a delicate and very mild sweet licorice flavor. If you happen to find fennel with the feathery, dill-like tops still attached, chop some to use as a garnish. This is not a thickened chowder, so if you prefer a thicker consistency, try pureeing half of the soup and mixing it with the un-pureed half.

MAKES 8 SERVINGS

¼ cup unsalted butter

2½ cups diced leeks, white and light green parts

1¼ cups finely diced onion

2 tbsp minced shallot

1½ cups diced fennel

6 cups chicken or vegetable broth

4 cups diced yellow or white potatoes

1 cup heavy cream or half-and-half, heated

Salt as needed

Freshly ground white pepper as needed

6 tbsp minced chives or sliced scallions

1. Melt the butter in a soup pot over medium heat. Add the leeks, onion, shallot, and fennel; stir to coat evenly with butter. Cover and cook until the onion is tender and translucent, 4 to 5 minutes.

2. Add the broth and potatoes. Bring to a simmer and cook, stirring occasionally and skimming the surface as necessary, until the potatoes are tender, 20 to 25 minutes.

3. Add the cream, blend well, and return to a simmer. Adjust the seasoning to taste with salt and white pepper. Serve in heated bowls, garnished with the chives or scallions.

french lentil soup

THE EARTHY flavor of lentils is brightened by Riesling and sherry wine vinegar in this refined lentil soup. It is a brothy soup, but if you'd like it to have a thicker consistency, you can puree half the soup and combine it with the unpureed half. If you store this soup in the refrigerator, it may become thicker. Adjust the consistency as necessary by adding more broth and be sure to recheck the seasoning.

MAKES 8 SERVINGS

2 tbsp vegetable oil

1¼ cups finely diced onion

½ tsp minced garlic

⅔ cup finely diced carrots

1¼ cups finely diced leek, white and light green parts

½ cup finely diced celery

1 tbsp tomato paste

7 cups chicken or vegetable broth

1¾ cups French (green) lentils

¼ cup Riesling or other slightly sweet white wine

2 tbsp sherry wine vinegar

½ lemon

Sachet: 2 sprigs fresh thyme or 1 tsp dried, 1 bay leaf, and ¼ tsp caraway seeds enclosed in a large tea ball or tied in a cheesecloth pouch

½ tsp salt, or as needed

¼ tsp freshly ground white pepper, or as needed

1. Heat the oil in a soup pot over medium heat. Add the onion and garlic. Cook, stirring occasionally, until the onion is translucent, 4 to 6 minutes. Add the carrots, leek, and celery. Cook, stirring occasionally until the vegetables have softened, 5 to 7 minutes. Add the tomato paste, stirring well until blended, and cook for 2 more minutes.

2. Add the remaining ingredients and bring to a simmer. Cook until the lentils are tender, about 40 minutes. Remove and discard the sachet and lemon half.

3. Adjust the seasoning to taste with salt and pepper. Serve in heated bowls.

french onion soup

THE SECRET to making a fine French onion soup is to give it lots of time to develop flavor. The onions should be cooked slowly until they become deeply caramelized. Then they should be simmered in broth for nearly an hour to allow their flavors to permeate the broth. If you have the time, we recommend you make the soup the day before you serve it to allow the flavor to mature and mellow. Taking this route will also give you the opportunity to lift away any excess fat that has solidified on the surface.

MAKES 8 SERVINGS

¼ cup olive or vegetable oil

5 cups thinly sliced onions

1 tsp minced garlic

½ cup brandy

6 cups beef or chicken broth, heated

Sachet: 3 to 4 parsley stems, ½ tsp each dried thyme and tarragon, and 1 bay leaf enclosed in a large tea ball or tied in a cheesecloth pouch

Salt as needed

Freshly ground black pepper as needed

8 slices French bread

1 cup grated Gruyère cheese, or more as needed

1. Heat the oil in a soup pot over medium-low heat. Add the onions and cook without stirring until the onions begin to brown on the bottom. Raise the heat to medium, stir, and continue to cook, stirring occasionally, until the onions are deeply caramelized (dark golden brown). The total cooking time will be 30 to 45 minutes. If the onions begin to scorch, add a few tablespoons of water and continue cooking.

2. Add the garlic and continue to cook for an additional minute. Add the brandy and simmer until the liquid has nearly evaporated, 2 to 3 minutes.

3. Add the broth and sachet. Bring to a simmer and cook, partially covered, for 45 minutes to 1 hour, skimming the surface as necessary and discarding the fat. Remove and discard the sachet. Season to taste with salt and pepper.

4. When ready to serve the soup, preheat the broiler. Ladle the soup into individual ovenproof soup crocks. Top each crock with 1 slice of bread and sprinkle with enough of the grated cheese to cover the bread completely, allowing the cheese to touch the edge of the crock.

5. Place the soup crocks in a large baking dish and broil until the soup is thoroughly heated and the cheese is lightly browned, 2 to 3 minutes. Serve immediately.

goulash soup

REMINISCENT OF the paprika-flavored Hungarian stew of the same name (spelled *gulyás* in Hungarian), this is a thick and robust soup. Serve it with a dab of sour cream, if you wish, and accompany it with lots of dark pumpernickel bread and dark beer.

MAKES 8 SERVINGS

6 tbsp minced salt pork, slab bacon, or fatback

1 lb beef or veal chuck, cut into ½-inch cubes

2½ cups finely diced onion

2 tbsp red wine vinegar

2 tbsp all-purpose flour

1 tbsp hot paprika

¾ cup tomato puree

4 cups beef broth

Sachet: 1 tsp each caraway seeds, dried marjoram, and thyme, 4 parsley stems, 2 peeled garlic cloves, and 1 bay leaf enclosed in a large tea ball or tied in a cheesecloth pouch

2 cups diced yellow or white potatoes

Salt as needed

Freshly ground black pepper as needed

¼ cup finely sliced scallion greens or chives

1. Sauté the salt pork in a soup pot over medium heat until the bits of pork are crisp and the fat has rendered, 4 to 5 minutes. Add the cubed beef or veal and sauté in the fat until the meat begins to brown, 3 to 4 minutes. Add the onion and cook, covered, over medium-low heat until the onion is translucent, 8 to 10 minutes.

2. Add the vinegar and bring to a boil over high heat. Continue to boil until the liquid begins to reduce in volume, about 2 minutes. Reduce the heat to medium. Using a wooden spoon, stir in the flour and cook for 1 more minute. Stir in the paprika, then the tomato puree, and mix thoroughly; cook for 2 to 3 minutes.

3. Add the broth and the sachet. Bring the soup to a simmer and cook until the meat is almost tender, about 30 minutes. Add the diced potatoes and simmer until tender, about 20 minutes. Remove and discard the sachet. Skim away any fat on the surface of the soup with a shallow spoon.

4. Season to taste with salt and pepper. Serve in heated bowls, garnished with the sliced scallions or chives.

dried beef soup

Caldo de Carne Seca

U SING DRIED beef, or *carne seca*, adds complexity to this rich, savory dish. We've included instructions to make your own carne seca, essentially a type of beef jerky. If you use purchased dried beef, you may need to soak it in warm water to cover for 15 minutes to remove some of the salt.

SERVES 8

2 tbsp olive oil or lard

1½ cups thinly sliced onion

1 tsp minced garlic

¾ lb carne seca (dried beef), diced or cut into strips (see note)

2 cups chopped plum tomatoes, fresh or canned

½ cup chopped cilantro

8 cups beef broth

1 cup medium-dice potatoes

½ cup medium-dice carrots

Salt as needed

Freshly ground black pepper as needed

1. Heat a soup pot over medium heat. Add the olive oil or lard. When the fat is shimmering, add the onion and sauté, stirring occasionally, until it is tender and a deep golden brown, 12 to 15 minutes. Add the garlic and continue to sauté until aromatic, 30 to 40 seconds.

2. Add the beef, tomatoes, and cilantro, stir well to coat with the oil or lard, and sauté for an additional 3 minutes. Add the broth, potatoes, and carrots and bring the soup to a boil, skimming the surface, as needed. Reduce the heat slightly, and simmer the soup until the carrots are tender, 25 to 30 minutes. Season to taste with salt and pepper.

3. Serve the soup in heated bowls.

MAKING CARNE SECA

To make your own carne seca, trim a 3-pound piece of boneless beef round to remove all surface fat. Use a slicer to cut the meat into thin slices, about ⅛-inch-thick. If you partially freeze the meat, it is easier to slice thinly.

Blend ¼ cup each of lime juice and soy sauce, and then add 1 tablespoon kosher salt, 1 tablespoon chili powder, 2 teaspoons of onion powder, and 2 teaspoons of garlic powder in a bowl. Add the sliced beef and turn to coat it evenly. Let the meat marinate for 30 minutes.

Preheat an oven (use a convection oven if you have one) to 175°F. Arrange the meat slices in a single layer on racks set on baking sheets or pans. Dry the meat in the preheated oven until it is thoroughly dried and leathery, 1 to 2 hours (depending upon the thickness of your slices.) Refrigerate until needed.

ham bone and collard greens soup

THIS HEARTY southern-style soup is packed with vitamin- and mineral-rich collard greens. Ham Bone Soup was originally a means of getting the most meal mileage from a ham, but we have developed this recipe using a smoked ham hock (which should be available from your supermarket), so you don't have to purchase and eat a whole ham to make the soup. If you do happen to have a meaty ham bone, though, by all means use it instead of the ham hock. Ham hocks can be quite salty, so use salt-free homemade broth or a reduced-sodium canned variety to make this soup.

MAKES 8 SERVINGS

1 smoked ham hock

12 cups chicken broth

1¼ lb collard greens

1 tbsp vegetable oil

¼ cup minced salt pork

1¼ cups minced onion

½ cup minced celery

½ cup all-purpose flour

Sachet: 5 to 6 black peppercorns, 4 parsley stems, 1 fresh thyme sprig or ½ tsp dried enclosed in a large tea ball or tied in a cheesecloth pouch

½ cup heavy cream

4 tsp malt vinegar, or as needed

Tabasco sauce as needed

1. Place the ham hock and broth in a pot large enough to accommodate both. Bring to a simmer and cook, partially covered, for 1½ hours. Remove the ham hock from the broth and allow both to cool slightly.

2. Bring a large pot of salted water to a boil. Cut the tough ribs and stems away from the collard greens and discard. Plunge the greens into the boiling water and cook for 10 minutes. Drain and cool slightly. Chop the greens coarsely and set aside.

3. Heat the oil in a soup pot over medium heat. Add the salt pork and cook until crisp, 3 to 5 minutes. Add the onion and celery and cook, stirring occasionally, until tender, about 5 minutes.

4. Add the flour and cook, stirring frequently, for 5 minutes. Gradually add the broth, whisking constantly to work out any lumps of flour, and bring to a simmer. Add the collard greens, ham hock, and sachet; simmer for 1 hour.

5. Remove and discard the sachet. Remove the ham hock and cool slightly. Trim away the skin and fat and discard. Dice the lean meat, and return it to the soup.

6. Add the cream and season to taste with the vinegar and Tabasco. Serve in heated bowls.

HOMEMADE CROUTONS

Homemade croutons enliven any salad or soup with a satisfying crunch. If you prefer, slice the baguettes into thin slices instead of making cubes for a different effect or to use as a base for a canapé or crostini.

Toss 4 cups of cubed bread with 2 tbsp olive oil, or more if you need it. Use a pastry brush to spread the oil lightly on slices of bread you plan to make into large croutons or crostini. Season the oiled bread with salt and freshly ground black pepper, as well as any flavorings you want to add: a pinch fresh or dried herbs (rosemary, oregano, and chives are all

senate bean soup

ACCORDING TO legend, when this soup disappeared from the U.S. Senate dining room menu with the approach of hot weather, there was such an outcry that it was soon restored. Just to be certain that they would never be without their favorite soup again, the Senate passed a bill requiring that it be offered every day that the dining hall was open.

MAKES 8 SERVINGS

1¼ cups dried navy beans

2 tbsp olive oil

¾ cup finely diced carrot

1 cup finely diced celery

½ tsp minced garlic

¾ cup finely diced onion

4 cups chicken or vegetable broth

1 smoked ham hock

1 cup diced yellow or white potato

Sachet: 3 to 4 whole black peppercorns and 1 whole clove enclosed in a large tea ball or tied in a cheesecloth pouch

Salt as needed

Freshly ground white pepper as needed

Tabasco sauce as needed

1 cup Homemade Croutons, flavored with garlic (see recipe below)

1. Sort through the beans, discarding any stones or bad beans. Place the beans in a large pot and pour in enough water to cover them by at least 3 inches. Bring to a boil, and then remove the pot from the heat. Cover and allow the beans to soak for 1 hour. Drain the beans, rinse them in cold water, and set aside.

2. Heat the oil in a soup pot over medium heat. Add the carrot, celery, garlic, and onion. Cook over low to medium heat until the garlic has a sweet aroma and the onion is a light golden brown, about 5 minutes. Add the beans, broth, and ham hock. If necessary, add enough water to cover the beans by about 1 inch. Bring to a simmer, cover, and cook for 1 hour.

3. Add the potato and sachet. Continue to simmer the soup over low heat until the beans and potatoes are tender enough to mash easily, about 30 minutes.

4. Remove the ham hock from the soup. When it is cool enough to handle easily, pull the lean meat away from the bone and dice it. Reserve this meat to add to the soup as a garnish. Remove and discard the sachet.

5. Puree about half of the soup until smooth. Add this back to the remainder of the soup. If necessary, thin the soup with additional broth. Season to taste with salt, pepper, and Tabasco sauce. Serve the soup in heated bowls or cups, garnished with the diced ham and croutons.

good choices), minced garlic, or grated Parmesan cheese, for instance. You can substitute any number of different combinations of these seasonings, or omit the seasonings altogether for plain croutons.

Preheat the oven to 350°F. Spread the croutons in an even layer on a baking sheet. Bake until golden brown, stirring occasionally so the croutons bake evenly, 10 to 12 minutes (baking time varies depending upon the size of the bread cubes). Allow to cool. Croutons will keep well in an airtight container for several days.

tunisian-style vegetable and bean soup

Hlelem

PACKED WITH beans and greens, this slightly spicy vegetable soup is both tasty and good for you. Harissa is a Tunisian hot sauce or paste usually made with hot chiles, garlic, cumin, coriander, caraway, and olive oil. It's available in cans, jars, or tubes from Middle Eastern markets and specialty stores, but it is easy to make your own.

MAKES 8 SERVINGS

½ cup dried lima or butter beans

½ cup dried chick peas

2 tbsp olive oil

1 tsp minced garlic

½ cup diced celery

¾ cup minced onion

4 cups chicken broth

⅓ cup tomato paste

4 large Swiss chard leaves, stems removed and cut
    into 1-inch pieces, leaves shredded

⅓ cup angel hair pasta, broken into bite-size pieces

2 tbsp Harissa (page 143)

Salt as needed

Freshly ground black pepper as needed

½ cup chopped parsley

1. Soak the dried lima beans and chick peas separately overnight in three times their volume of cold water. Drain and cook them separately in two times their volume of fresh water until they are tender, about 45 minutes. Drain and reserve the cooking water from both the lima beans and the chick peas. Combine the lima beans and chick peas; set aside. Combine the cooking waters and set aside.

2. Heat the olive oil in a soup pot over medium heat. Add the garlic, celery, and onion. Cook, stirring occasionally, until the onion is translucent, 4 to 6 minutes.

3. Add the broth, 3 cups of the reserved bean cooking liquid, and the tomato paste, stirring until well blended, and bring to a simmer. Continue to simmer for 10 minutes.

4. Approximately 10 minutes before serving, add the cooked beans and chick peas, the Swiss chard, and the pasta. Add more of the reserved bean cooking liquid as necessary. Simmer until the pasta and chard stems are tender, about 10 minutes.

5. Add the harissa and stir until blended. Season to taste with salt and pepper. Serve in heated bowls, garnished with the chopped parsley.

tunisian chick pea soup

Leblebi

𝒴OU CAN substitute 3½ cups of drained and rinsed canned chick peas for the dried; add them along with the garlic spice paste and harissa.

MAKES 6 SERVINGS

2 tbsp olive oil

1 medium onion, diced

1½ cups dried chick peas, soaked overnight in 1 quart of water

8 cups vegetable or chicken broth

1 tsp toasted cumin seeds

½ tsp salt, plus more as needed

5 garlic cloves, coarsely chopped

1 tsp Harissa (page 143)

Freshly ground black pepper as needed

Three 1-inch-thick slices of day old French bread,
    cut into 1-inch cubes

Garnishes (see note)

1. Heat the oil in a skillet over medium heat. Add the onion and cook until translucent, 6 to 8 minutes. Set aside.

2. Drain the soaking liquid from the chick peas and place them in a large saucepan or a soup pot. Add the broth and bring to a simmer. Cover and simmer gently for 20 minutes.

3. Crush the cumin seeds with ½ teaspoon salt in a mortar. Add the garlic and crush to a paste. Add the garlic/spice paste and the harissa to the soup. Continue to simmer until the chick peas are barely tender, 15 to 20 minutes.

4. Add the onion, along with the olive oil it was cooked in, and simmer until the chick peas are fully tender, about 15 minutes. Season to taste with salt and pepper.

5. To serve, divide the bread chunks equally between the heated soup bowls. Ladle about ½ cup of broth into each bowl. Arrange the garnishes in small bowls or on a tray with additional salt and pepper. Once the bread has softened, add the chick peas to the soup bowls. Serve immediately with the garnishes and the olive oil.

GARNISHES FOR LEBLEBI

Try one or more of these garnishes for the soup:

2 hard-cooked eggs, coarsely chopped

2 lemons, quartered

One 6-oz can tuna, drained and flaked

½ cup thinly sliced scallion (white and green parts)

½ cup coarsely chopped capers, drained

⅓ cup Harissa (page 143)

Ground cumin as needed

Cruet of extra-virgin olive oil

paraguayan dumpling soup

Bori-Bori

bORI-BORI IS a hearty soup from Paraguay made with meat, vegetables, and cornmeal-cheese dumplings. Just a few threads of the optional saffron will give the soup a rich golden color.

SERVES 8

2 tbsp canola oil or bacon fat

1 lb boneless beef shank

Salt as needed

Freshly ground black pepper as needed

8 cups chicken broth, plus as needed

1½ cups minced onion

¾ cup small-dice carrot

¾ cup small-dice celery

2 tsp minced garlic

1 bay leaf

1 whole clove

2 or 3 crushed saffron threads, optional

Parmesan-Cornmeal Dumplings (recipe follows)

3 tbsp chopped flat-leaf parsley

¼ cup grated Parmesan cheese

1. Heat 1 tablespoon of the oil in a soup pot over medium-high heat. Season the beef shank with salt and pepper and add it to the hot oil. Sear the beef on all sides, turning as necessary, until browned, 7 to 8 minutes.

2. Add the chicken broth and simmer over low heat until the beef is tender, 45 to 50 minutes. Remove the beef to a plate and let cool. Strain the broth through a fine sieve and reserve. (Make the dumpling batter while the soup simmers to give it enough time to rest.)

3. Return the soup pot to medium-high heat. Add the remaining oil and heat over medium-high heat. Add the onion, carrot, celery, and garlic and sauté, stirring frequently, until the onion is tender and translucent, 8 to 10 minutes.

4. Add the strained broth to the soup pot along with additional chicken broth, if needed, to make 8 cups. Bring the broth to a simmer and add the bay leaf, clove, and saffron threads, if using. Simmer until the vegetables are tender and the broth is flavorful, 30 minutes. Remove the bay leaf and clove and discard.

5. Trim the cooled beef and cut it into medium dice. Return the beef to the soup. Add the dumplings and simmer the soup until the dumplings are cooked through, 20 to 25 minutes. Stir in the parsley, and season to taste with salt and pepper. Serve immediately in warmed soup bowls sprinkled with Parmesan cheese.

Parmesan-Cornmeal Dumplings

SERVES 8

⅓ cup white or yellow cornmeal

⅓ cup grated Parmesan cheese

¼ cup all-purpose flour

½ tsp baking powder

½ tsp salt

Pinch of freshly ground black pepper

1 large egg, lightly beaten

2 tbsp minced scallions, white portion only

1 tbsp canola oil

(recipe method continues on page 30)

1. Using a fork, combine the cornmeal, Parmesan, flour, baking powder, salt, and pepper in a bowl. Add the egg, scallions, and oil and blend to form a dough. Turn the dough out onto a floured surface and knead until the dough is smooth, 3 to 4 minutes. Wipe out the bowl, return the dough to the bowl, cover with plastic, and let it rest for 45 minutes.

2. To form the dumplings, pinch off small pieces (about ½ teaspoon) and roll them into balls.

salmon miso soup

MISO, FERMENTED soybean paste, is a principle ingredient in Japanese cooking. It comes in a variety of flavors and colors. Most miso is quite salty, though low-salt varieties are available. It contains large amounts of protein and B vitamins, making it highly nutritious as well. The variety called for in this soup, yellow (shinshu) miso, is very mellow as misos go.

MAKES 8 SERVINGS

3 tsp vegetable oil

1 egg, lightly beaten

3 tbsp thinly sliced scallion greens

½ tsp minced fresh ginger

¼ cup diced carrot

¼ cup diced daikon

6 cups chicken broth

5 tbsp yellow miso

2¼ tsp instant dashi

¼ cup dried wakame seaweed, broken into 1-inch pieces, optional

1 cup diced soft tofu

½ cup finely diced fresh boneless, skinless salmon fillet (about 3 oz)

2¼ tsp dark (Asian) sesame oil

¼ tsp freshly ground black pepper

1. Heat 1 teaspoon of the oil in a nonstick omelet pan or small skillet over medium-low heat. Add the beaten egg and cook until set on the bottom, about 1 minute. Flip the omelet and cook until completely set, 1 to 2 minutes. Transfer the omelet to a cutting board, dice, and set aside.

2. Heat the remaining 2 teaspoons of oil in a large wok or soup pot. Add half of the scallion greens and the ginger. Stir-fry briefly, about 30 seconds. Add the carrot and daikon. Stir-fry until tender, about 3 minutes.

3. Add the chicken broth, miso, and instant dashi, stirring until completely dissolved. Add the seaweed, if using. Bring the soup to a simmer. Add the tofu, salmon, sesame oil, and black pepper. Simmer until the salmon is just cooked, about 1 minute.

4. Serve in heated bowls, garnished with the remaining scallions and diced omelet.

minestrone

MINESTRONE, LITERALLY "big soup," is an Italian classic packed with vegetables, pasta, and beans. There is no one right way to make minestrone. Recipes vary from cook to cook according to individual preferences, so feel free to improvise with other vegetables, beans, or pasta shapes to suit your taste. Pancetta is a type of Italian bacon. It can usually be found in delis and butcher shops, but if it is unavailable in your area, you can omit it or substitute regular bacon.

MAKES 8 SERVINGS

2 tbsp olive oil

1 slice pancetta (or 2 strips bacon), chopped

1½ cups chopped green cabbage

1 cup chopped onion

1 cup sliced carrot

¼ cup chopped celery

2 garlic cloves, minced

8 cups chicken broth

½ cup peeled, diced potato

One 3-inch piece Parmesan cheese rind (see note, page 30)

¾ cup vermicelli or angel hair pasta, broken into 2-inch pieces

½ cup chopped plum tomatoes

¼ cup drained canned chick peas

⅓ cup drained canned kidney beans

⅓ cup pesto (recipe follows)

Salt as needed

Freshly ground black pepper as needed

Freshly grated Parmesan cheese as needed

1. Heat the oil in a soup pot over medium heat. Add the pancetta and cook until the fat melts, 3 to 5 minutes. Do not allow the pancetta to brown. Add the cabbage, onion, carrot, celery, and garlic. Cook until the onion is translucent, about 6 to 8 minutes.

2. Add the broth, potato, and Parmesan cheese rind. Bring to a simmer and cook until the vegetables are tender, about 30 minutes. Do not overcook them.

3. Meanwhile, cook the vermicelli according to package directions until tender; drain and reserve.

4. When the vegetables in the soup are tender, add the cooked vermicelli, tomatoes, chick peas, and kidney beans. Cook just until heated through. Remove and discard the Parmesan rind.

5. Season the soup to taste with the pesto, salt, and pepper. Serve in heated bowls, sprinkled with Parmesan cheese.

Pesto

MAKES 1 CUP

2 cups packed basil leaves

3 garlic cloves, peeled

Zest and juice of 1 lemon

5 tbsp toasted pine nuts

⅔ cup grated Parmesan cheese

¼ tsp salt

¼ tsp freshly ground black pepper

¼ to ⅓ cup extra-virgin olive oil

Combine the basil, garlic, lemon juice and zest, pine nuts, Parmesan, salt, and pepper in a food processor, pulse until finely chopped. Add ¼ cup of the olive oil in a thin stream until fully incorporated and a thick paste forms; add more olive oil if necessary.

mulligatawny soup

For the best flavor, grind the spices fresh yourself. If you like, you can substitute chicken for the lamb without sacrificing authenticity.

MAKES 8 SERVINGS

1 or 2 jalapeño peppers

4 tsp ground black pepper

1 tbsp ground coriander

2 tsp ground turmeric

¾ tsp ground cumin

½ tsp ground nutmeg

¼ tsp ground cloves

5 garlic cloves

2 tsp grated or minced ginger root

2 tbsp butter

2½ cups diced onion

1 lb lamb stew meat, cut into ½-inch cubes

8 cups chicken broth

⅓ cup tomato paste

1½ tsp salt

⅔ cup diced carrot

1½ cups diced apple

¾ cup diced potato

½ cup frozen peas

Lemon slices, optional

1. Remove the stems from the jalapeño(s). For a milder spice level, remove the seeds as well. Grind the jalapeño(s), black pepper, coriander, turmeric, cumin, nutmeg, cloves, garlic, and ginger to a paste in a blender or mortar and pestle.

2. Heat the butter in a soup pot over medium heat. Add the onion and cook, stirring occasionally, until golden brown, about 10 minutes. Add the spice paste and cubed lamb, and cook for 5 minutes.

3. Add the broth, tomato paste, and salt; bring to a simmer. Continue to simmer for 20 minutes. Add the carrot, apple, and potato. Continue to simmer the soup until everything is tender, another 20 minutes.

4. Add the peas and simmer just until heated through, about 5 minutes. Serve the soup in heated bowls, garnished with lemon slices, if using.

PEPPER WATER

Mulligatawny soup is a product of the British colonization of India. The British required a separate soup course with their meals, but the Indian custom was to serve all the foods in a meal at one time. Furthermore, the closest dishes to soup in Indian cuisine at that time were used as thin sauces poured over rice or dry curries. They were never drunk by themselves. Mulligatawny was born of this need. The name, which is a corruption of "milagu-tannir," comes from the Tamil people of southern India. It means "pepper water," hence the large amount of black pepper in the recipe.

petite marmite

SOME PEOPLE serve the broth as a first course with the meats and vegetables following; others present the meats and vegetables as the soup's garnish (the approach suggested here). Add some crusty bread and either way you serve it, this soup makes a healthy and hearty meal.

MAKES 8 SERVINGS

1 whole chicken (about 3 lb)

1½ lb beef bottom round

12 cups chicken broth

1 cup diced celery

1½ cups diced leeks, white and light green parts

1½ cups diced onion

½ cup diced carrot

1 cup diced purple-top turnip

2 cups shredded white or green cabbage

Sachet: 1 bay leaf, ¼ tsp dried thyme, 4 black peppercorns, 4 parsley stems, 1 peeled garlic clove enclosed in a large tea ball or tied in a cheesecloth pouch

Salt as needed

Freshly ground black pepper as needed

¼ cup chopped parsley

1½ cups Homemade Croutons (page 24)

1. Remove the neck and giblets from the cavity of the chicken. Rinse the cavity with cold water. Place the beef and chicken in a large soup pot. Add the cold broth to cover, and bring to a simmer over low heat. With a shallow flat spoon, skim off the foam as it rises to the surface and discard. Simmer until the beef and chicken are fork-tender, about 2 hours.

2. Remove the beef and chicken and set aside to cool. Strain the broth through a cheesecloth-lined sieve. Return the broth to the soup pot. Add the celery, leeks, onion, carrot, turnip, cabbage, and sachet to the broth. Bring to a simmer and cook until the vegetables are tender, 15 to 20 minutes. Remove and discard the sachet.

3. When the beef and chicken have cooled, remove the gristle from the beef and dice. Remove the skin and bones from the chicken. Dice the chicken meat. Return the beef and the chicken to the broth. Simmer for an additional 5 minutes to heat thoroughly. Season to taste with salt and pepper. Serve in heated bowls, garnished with parsley and croutons.

THE GLOBAL SOUP POT

When it comes to having their own dinner, many professional chefs like nothing better than a big bowl of petite marmite, a heavenly broth full of meat, poultry, and vegetables. Though named and claimed by the French, this soup can be found in one form or another in virtually every cuisine, although the aromatic flavorings and the presentation may vary.

Some people do not consider a Petite Marmite to be authentic unless it contains diced marrow. To add the marrow, first soak 1 pound of marrow bones in cold water for several hours; rinse well. Place the bones in a pot,

cover with cold water, and bring to a simmer. Cook until the marrow can easily be scooped out of the bone with a spoon, 45 minutes to 1 hour. Dice the marrow and add it to the broth when you add the diced meat and poultry.

You may also substitute any of the following meats for, or combine them with, the beef and chicken: venison or other game meats, oxtails, pheasant or other game birds, turkey, ham hocks, pork, or lamb. The total weight should be about 4 pounds. Increase the broth as needed to cover the meats completely and follow the method above.

vegetable soup with radish salsa

Clemole con Salsa de Rábanos

THE RADISH salsa in this dish is a traditional offering in parts of Mexico and South America. In Oaxaca, Mexico, elaborate sculptures carved from radishes are displayed each year on December 23rd, The Night of the Radishes.

SERVES 6

SALSA DE RÁBANOS

1 cup water

4 tsp salt

1 tbsp red wine vinegar

1 cup finely chopped radishes

½ cup minced onion

¾ cup orange juice

½ cup lime juice

1½ lb tomatillos, husks removed, quartered

1 cup chopped cilantro

3 serrano chiles, stem and seeds removed, chopped

1½ lb boneless pork loin

10 cups water

1½ cups minced onion

2 tsp minced garlic

Salt as needed

Freshly ground black pepper as needed

3 ears of corn, husked and cut into 3 pieces

1½ cups sliced zucchini

1½ cups green beans, trimmed and cut into ½-inch-long pieces

1. To make the salsa, combine 1 cup of water, the salt, and the vinegar in a bowl. Add the radishes, onion, orange, and lime juice. Cover tightly and let the salsa rest in the refrigerator at least 1 and up to 3 hours before serving.

2. Puree the tomatillos, cilantro, and serranos to a coarse paste in a food processor or blender. Set aside.

3. Trim the pork loin and cut it into large cubes. Place it in a large soup pot, and add the water (there should be enough to cover the pork by at least 2 inches), the onion, and garlic. Bring to a boil over high heat, skimming any foam that rises to the surface. As soon as a full boil is reached, reduce the heat and simmer the pork, covered, until the pork is tender, about 45 minutes. Season to taste with salt and pepper.

4. Add the corn, zucchini, and green beans to the soup. Continue to simmer until all the vegetables are tender, 10 to 15 minutes. Just before serving, remove the soup from the heat, and stir in the tomatillos mixture. Season to taste with salt and pepper.

5. Serve the soup in heated bowls topped with the salsa.

tortilla soup

This soup, fragrant with the aromas of cilantro, chili powder, and cumin, is both flavored and thickened with corn tortillas. Toasting the tortillas before grinding them helps develop the fullest flavor. Garnished with avocado, cheese, chicken, and toasted tortilla strips, this soup is a delicious light meal.

MAKES 6 SERVINGS

4 corn tortillas

2 tsp vegetable oil

¾ cup finely grated or pureed onion

½ tsp minced garlic

¾ cup tomato puree

1 tbsp chopped cilantro leaves

1½ tsp mild chili powder

1 tsp ground cumin

6 cups chicken broth

1 bay leaf

1 cup shredded cooked chicken breast

2 tbsp grated Cheddar cheese

½ cup diced avocado (see note at right)

1. Preheat the oven to 300°F. Cut the tortillas into matchsticks. Place them in an even layer on a baking sheet and toast them in the oven for about 15 minutes. Or, toast the strips by sautéing them in a dry skillet over medium heat, tossing frequently. Reserve about ½ cup of the strips for a garnish. Crush the remainder in a food processor or blender.

2. Heat the oil in a soup pot over medium heat. Add the onion and garlic and cook, stirring frequently, until they release a sweet aroma, 5 to 6 minutes. Add the tomato puree and continue to cook for another 3 minutes. Add the cilantro, chili powder, and cumin and cook for another 2 minutes.

3. Add the broth, crushed tortillas, and bay leaf and bring the soup to a simmer, stirring well. Continue to simmer for 25 to 30 minutes. Strain the soup through a sieve, and serve immediately in heated bowls, garnished with the shredded chicken, Cheddar cheese, reserved tortilla strips, and diced avocado.

WORKING WITH AVOCADOS

Avocado will turn brown if it is cut very far in advance. Avoid cutting the avocado more than 1 hour before you will need it. Once you cut it, sprinkle the diced flesh with a little lemon or lime juice and toss gently to coat all the pieces. Cover the avocado and keep refrigerated. If avocados are not in season or unavailable, substitute peeled, seeded, and diced tomatoes or cucumbers.

gazpacho

HIS TANGY marriage of fresh tomato, cucumber, pepper, and onion is a summer favorite. The flavor of gazpacho improves if allowed to chill overnight, but thereafter this soup has a short shelf life because the tomatoes sour very quickly. It is best prepared no more than a day or two before it will be eaten.

MAKES 8 SERVINGS

3 cups finely diced plum tomatoes, juices reserved

2 cups finely diced cucumbers, peeled and seeded

1¼ cups finely diced onion

1 cup finely diced red bell pepper

1 tsp minced garlic

2 tbsp tomato paste

2 tbsp extra-virgin olive oil

2 tbsp minced fresh herbs (tarragon, thyme, or parsley)

3 cups canned tomato juice

¼ cup red wine vinegar, or as needed

Juice of ½ lemon, or as needed

¼ tsp salt, or as needed

¼ tsp cayenne pepper, or as needed

1 cup tiny croutons

½ cup thinly sliced chives or scallion greens

1. Reserve 2 tablespoons each of the tomatoes, cucumbers, onion, and pepper for the garnish.

2. Puree the remaining tomato, cucumber, onion, and pepper in a food processor or blender along with the garlic, tomato paste, olive oil, and herbs until fairly smooth but with some texture remaining.

3. Transfer the puree to a mixing bowl. Stir in the tomato juice, the red wine vinegar, and lemon juice. Season with salt and cayenne to taste. Cover and chill thoroughly, at least 3 hours but preferably overnight.

4. After chilling, check the seasoning and adjust as needed. Serve in chilled bowls, garnished with the reserved vegetables, croutons, and chives.

MAKING THIS RECIPE YOURS

If the soup is too thin for your taste, add about 1 cup of freshly made white bread crumbs before chilling. If it's too thick, the consistency can be thinned by adding more tomato juice or water. Part of the tomato juice can be replaced with fish broth or clam juice, if desired.

chile and cheese soup

Minguichi

THIS SOUP is perfect at the end of summer when the tomatoes and corn are at their best, but it's just as flavorful in the winter, and even quicker to make from canned tomatoes and frozen corn. If you wish, you can stir the cheese into the soup just before you serve it, but we like the way the heat of the soup melts the cheese while you eat it.

SERVES 6

3 cups seeded and quartered plum tomatoes

1 tbsp canola oil

2 tsp butter

2 cups minced onion

2 tsp minced garlic

4 cups corn kernels, thawed if frozen

2 tsp salt

½ tsp freshly ground black pepper

4 cups chicken broth

2 roasted poblano chiles, peeled, seeded,
    cut into strips (see page 9)

½ cup milk

½ cup heavy cream

5 oz queso manchego (or Muenster)

1. Puree the tomatoes through a food mill or in a blender and reserve.

2. Heat the oil in a soup pot over medium heat. Add the butter and melt it. Add the onion and garlic and sauté, stirring occasionally, until the onion is tender and translucent, 8 to 10 to minutes. Add the corn and sauté until heated through, 5 to 6 minutes.

3. Add the pureed tomatoes and simmer for 5 minutes. Season to taste with salt and pepper. Add the broth and continue to simmer until the corn is tender and the soup is flavorful, 10 to 12 minutes. Add the roasted poblano strips and simmer until they flavor the soup, 5 minutes. Add the milk and cream and simmer until heated through, about 5 minutes.

4. Remove the soup from the heat. Divide the cheese equally between 6 warmed soup bowls. Ladle the hot soup over the cheese and serve at once.

stews

STEWING IS PERHAPS the quintessential one-pot method of cooking. Whether you are preparing hearty stews made from beef, game, or other meats, or lighter versions that feature vegetables or seafood, there are some basics that you should keep in mind.

Choose the Best Ingredients

For stews, this often means ingredients that are more mature and flavorful. If you are planning a beef stew, choose cuts from the shoulder or the shank for a deep rich taste. For poultry stews, you may need to use a stewing hen or fowl, or perhaps select leg or thigh meat rather than breast meat.

Cook the Stew Properly

A good stew is never cooked at a hard boil. Cooking a stew that hard and fast would result in a disappointing dish. For tender, melting textures and big, bold flavors, keep the stew at a bare simmer with just a few lazy bubbles bursting on the surface. If you wish, you can opt to finish stews in the oven. This has the effect of maintaining a slow, steady, even, and very gentle heat. The only caveat is that you need to be more vigilant about checking the dish as it stews. Once you move something from the stovetop into the oven, it is a little easier to forget about it. Use your kitchen timer to keep track of the stew as it cooks.

Flavor, Season, and Garnish the Stew Judiciously

You nearly always can add other ingredients to a stew as it simmers. If the ingredients you want to add are already cooked (beans, pasta, rice, potatoes, meats, and so forth), add them in the last few minutes of cooking time, just long enough for them to reheat. Other garnishes may need to be added earlier on, as the stew simmers, so that they finish cooking at the same time as the main ingredients. Add seasonings a little at a time throughout the cooking process. Adding just a little bit at a time gives you more control.

If you are simmering dry beans in the stew, don't add any salt or acidic ingredients like wine or vinegar until the beans are beginning to turn tender. Remember that the flavor of your stew will deepen as it cooks, but if you don't add seasonings throughout, the flavor may not have the depth you intended.

beef in mussaman curry sauce

Kaeng Mussaman

MUSSAMAN CURRY is the mildest of the Thai curries. You can find prepared curry pastes in large grocery stores or shops that specialize in Asian products, or you can make your own—see the sidebar below.

MAKES 4 SERVINGS

5 cups coconut milk

2 lb boneless beef chuck, cut in 2-inch chunks

⅓ cup Mussaman curry paste (or substitute red curry)

4 cups large-dice potatoes

3 tbsp fish sauce plus as needed

3 tbsp tamarind pulp (see page 2)

2 tbsp palm sugar plus as needed (see page 54)

6 cinnamon sticks

1 tsp ground cardamom

¾ cup large-dice yellow onion

½ cup pan-roasted peanuts

2 tsp lime juice or as needed

1. Heat the coconut milk in a large saucepot over medium heat until it comes to a gentle boil, about 10 minutes. Skim off any cream that rises to the surface and transfer it to a small, heavy bottomed saucepan or skillet.

2. Add the beef chunks to the coconut milk in the saucepot and continue to simmer until the beef is tender, about 1 hour.

3. Bring the coconut cream to a gentle boil over medium heat. Adjust the heat to maintain a gentle boil and cook, stirring occasionally, until the coconut cream becomes thick and fragrant and tiny pools of oil glisten on the surface, 6 to 8 minutes. Add the curry paste and stir to dissolve it in the coconut cream. Simmer the mixture until it has a rich aroma, 3 to 4 minutes.

4. Add the curry paste mixture to the beef and coconut milk; stir well. Add the potatoes, fish sauce, tamarind, palm sugar, cinnamon, and cardamom and simmer until the potatoes are par-cooked, about 10 minutes. Add the onion and peanuts and simmer until the potatoes are tender, about 5 minutes more. Season to taste with additional fish sauce, palm sugar, and lime juice. It should have a pleasing, sweet, sour, and salty balance.

MAKING MUSSAMAN CURRY PASTE

Mussaman curry paste , or phrik kang mussaman, has a distinct aroma, due to the number of spices it contains. It is usually based on dried chiles and contains coriander and cumin. The measurements given here are just are starting point. *(continues on page 44)*

CLOCKWISE FROM UPPER LEFT *Toasting the curry paste on the stove before adding the coconut milk will give depth of flavor to your finished dish. When stewing, make sure that the amount of liquid in the pot completely covers the items to be cooked. When toasting nuts, take care to keep the nuts in a single layer in the pan and stir them often so that they don't brown unevenly. The finished Beef in Mussaman Curry Sauce is shown here served with steamed white rice (see note, page 160), but it could also be paired with saffron rice or couscous.*

Toast 1 tbsp coriander seeds and 1 tsp each of cumin seeds, fennel seeds, and cloves in a dry skillet or wok over moderate heat until very fragrant, about 2 minutes. Immediately transfer the spices to a plate or bowl and set aside.

Remove the stems and seeds from the chiles. Soak the chiles and 2 pieces of dried galangal in ½ cup warm water for 20 minutes. Transfer the chiles and galangal to a mortar or a blender. Discard the soaking water.

Chop the tender inner portion of one stalk of lemongrass. Scrape the roots from a bunch of cilantro and add them to the chiles. Mince 6 or 7 garlic cloves and ¼ of a small yellow onion. Add the garlic and onion to the chiles, along with the spice mixture, 1 tsp shrimp paste, and ½ tsp each freshly ground black pepper and nutmeg. Grind to a smooth paste. (If you are using a blender, you might have to add a few teaspoons of water.)

Use the curry paste immediately or store it in a closed container in the refrigerator for up to 2 weeks or in the freezer for up to 6 months.

PAN-ROASTING NUTS

You can buy roasted peanuts and cashews to garnish some of our Southeast Asian stews like this curry. For the best flavor and texture, however, consider toasting your own. You use the same technique to pan-roast spices and seeds for a depth of flavor you simply can't find in store-bought spice blends.

Let a heavy-bottomed skillet or sauté pan get very hot over high heat. Add the nuts, spices, or seeds to the pan in an even layer. Swirl the pan gently to keep the ingredients in motion constantly. The aromas will open up and deepen dramatically.

Once the nuts, spices, or seeds begin to give off a noticeable aroma, keep a close eye on them. They can go from perfect to overdone in a few seconds. Pour them out of the pan into a bowl just before they are the shade of brown you want.

TOASTING CURRY PASTE

While we admit that cooking the curry paste in a separate pot does violate the concept of a one dish meal, we know what it difference it can make, whether you are using your handmade version or a good quality brand that you've purchased.

Let a saucepan get very hot over high heat. Add the paste to the pan and stir it constantly. The aromas will open up and deepen dramatically.

Add the coconut cream and stir well to blend the curry into the cream. It's ready to add to your simmering curry now.

bolivian beef stew

THERE ARE many variations of this spicy, slow cooking, one-pot meal. Serve it with warm corn bread and salad greens dressed with lemon juice. Adjust the amount of jalapeño pepper to suit your family and friends.

MAKES 4 SERVINGS

1 lb boneless lean beef round, cut into 2-inch cubes

Salt to taste

Freshly ground black pepper to taste

1 tbsp canola oil

2 cups diced yellow onion

½ cup chopped red or green bell pepper

1 jalapeño pepper, seeded, deveined, and chopped

2 cups chopped plum tomatoes, fresh or canned

1 cup low-sodium beef broth

2 cups diced acorn or winter squash

2 red potatoes, diced

2 small ears of corn, sliced into 1-inch-thick rounds

2 tbsp minced cilantro

1. Season the beef generously with salt and pepper.

2. Heat the oil in a Dutch oven or casserole over medium high heat until it shimmers. Sauté the beef in the oil, stirring frequently, until the beef is browned on all sides, 8 to 10 minutes. Transfer the beef to a pan and keep warm.

3. Return the same pan to the heat. Add the onion, bell pepper, and jalapeño. Sauté, stirring frequently, until the onion is lightly browned, 8 to 10 minutes. Add the tomatoes and broth. Bring the liquid to a boil, and reduce the heat to low. Return the beef and any juices it may have released to the casserole. Simmer, covered, stirring occasionally, until the beef is tender, 1 to 1½ hours. Season to taste as the stew simmers with additional salt and pepper.

4. Add the squash, potatoes, and corn to the stew. Simmer, covered, until the vegetables are tender, about 20 minutes. Season to taste with additional salt and pepper. Divide the stew evenly among 4 heated bowls, sprinkle each serving with some of the cilantro, and serve.

lamb khorma

1 AMB KHORMA is a sensuous curry made by simmering lamb pieces with yogurt and cream, and thickening the sauce with a cashew paste. If you can find goat or sheep's milk yogurt, it will make a discernable difference in the taste.

MAKES 8 SERVINGS

2½ lb boneless lamb leg, cut into 1½-inch cubes

Salt as needed

Ground white pepper as needed

1½ cups plain yogurt

2 tbsp minced ginger root

1 tbsp minced garlic

2 tsp ground cardamom

12 oz cashew nuts

¼ cup ghee (see sidebar below) or canola oil

3 cups small-dice yellow onion

1 tsp ground cumin

1 tsp ground cardamom

1 tsp ground fennel

2 tbsp ground coriander

6 Thai bird chiles, chopped, or to taste

⅓ cup chopped cilantro stems

1 cup heavy cream

½ cup chopped cilantro leaves

1 cup pan-roasted cashews (see note, page 44)

4 cups steamed saffron rice (see note, page 160)

1. Trim the lamb and cut it into large pieces. Season with salt and pepper and put in a bowl. Add the yogurt, 1 tbsp ginger, the garlic, and cardamom. Stir or toss until the ingredients are evenly distributed and the lamb is coated. Cover and refrigerate for at least 30 minutes and up to 3 hours.

2. Put the cashews in a small bowl and add enough hot water to cover them. Let the cashews soak for 30 minutes and then drain. Grind the drained cashews to a coarse paste in a food processor. Set aside.

3. Heat the ghee or oil in a casserole or Dutch oven over medium heat until it shimmers. Add the onion and sauté until transparent, 6 to 8 minutes. Add the cumin, cardamom, fennel, the remaining ginger, and the coriander. Cook, stirring often until aromatic, about 2 minutes. Add the chiles, cilantro stems, and cashew paste and stir well to be sure that nothing is sticking. Sauté, stirring frequently and adding water a tablespoon at a time if necessary, until the mixture is very aromatic, about 2 minutes.

4. Add the lamb and the yogurt marinade, increase the heat, and stir until the pieces are evenly coated. Once the meat's juices begin to flow, reduce heat to low, cover, and simmer very slowly, stirring occasionally, until the meat is nearly tender, about 1½ hours.

5. Add the cream and continue to simmer until the curry is flavorful and thickened and the lamb is tender, 10 to 15 minutes. Season to taste with salt, pepper, and the Thai chiles. Garnish with cilantro leaves and cashews, and serve with saffron rice.

GHEE

Ghee, a type of cooking butter used in Indian cooking, can be purchased in jars at Asian or Indian markets, but it is easy to make yourself.

Cube 1 pound of cold unsalted butter, place in a saucepan, and set over low heat. Once the butter has melted, increase the heat slightly. The pure butterfat will become very clear. Some foam will rise to the top; skim it away.

Increase the heat slightly and continue to cook the butter until the milk solids that have fallen to the bottom of the pan turn a deep golden color.

Immediately remove the pan from the heat. Ladle the clear butterfat, or ghee, into a clean container; discard the liquid at the bottom of the pan. You can keep ghee in the refrigerator for up to 2 weeks.

lamb and pumpkin couscous

Use a *couscousière,* a type of nested pot specifically made for couscous, if you have one. If you don't have a couscousière, use a colander to hold the couscous over the stew as it simmers, as long as your pot's lid will trap enough of the steam with the colander in place, or make it separately. The couscous steams over the stew as it simmers. Follow the instructions on your couscous package.

MAKES 8 SERVINGS

¼ cup olive oil, or as needed

2 cups small-dice yellow onion

3 lb boneless lamb leg, cut into 1-inch cubes

Salt as needed

Freshly ground black pepper as needed

2 tsp ground ginger

1 tsp ground turmeric

½ tsp saffron threads, lightly crushed

8 cups chicken broth, as needed

3 cups cooked or canned chick-peas, drained

2 cups large-dice pumpkin or Hubbard squash

1 cup large-dice carrots

1 cup quartered purple-top turnips

Hoshaf as needed (recipe follows)

½ cup chopped cilantro

1. Heat the oil in the bottom of couscousière or in Dutch oven over high heat until it shimmers. Add the onion and sauté, stirring frequently, until tender and translucent, about 5 minutes. Season the lamb with salt and pepper and add it to the onion.

Continue to sauté, stirring frequently, until both the lamb and the onion have a deep brown color, about 10 minutes.

2. Add the ginger, turmeric, and saffron and continue to sauté until they have a toasted aroma, about 1 minute. Add the broth, adding enough to cover the lamb. Cover the casserole and simmer gently over low heat, stirring from time to time, until the lamb is nearly tender, about 45 minutes.

3. Add the chick peas, pumpkin, carrots, and turnips and continue simmering until the lamb and vegetables are very tender, about 30 minutes. (If desired, add couscous to the top of the couscousière or a colander and steam over the stew as directed on the package.) Add more broth or water if necessary to keep the ingredients covered as they stew.

4. Serve in heated plates, topped with Hoshaf and chopped cilantro.

Hoshaf

MAKES ½ CUP

24 medium-size dried apricots

6 cups water

¾ cup sugar

Soak the apricots in the water overnight. The next day, transfer the apricots and their soaking liquid to a saucepan and simmer over low heat for 30 minutes. Add the sugar, stirring slowly until sugar is dissolved, and simmer until thickened, 5 minutes. Remove from the heat and cool. Chop the apricots coarsely.

lamb navarin

THIS HEARTY French stew is traditionally prepared from mutton or lamb with a garnish of root vegetables, onions, and peas. The name probably derives from the French word for turnips, *navets*, an important ingredient in any true navarin. Rutabagas, also known as yellow turnips or Swedes, are perfect to use in this dish.

MAKES 4 TO 6 SERVINGS

3 lb boneless lamb shoulder, chuck, or brisket

Salt as needed

Freshly ground black pepper as needed

¼ cup vegetable oil

1 small yellow onion, diced

2 tbsp tomato paste

3 tbsp all-purpose flour

1½ cups beef broth

1 cup dry white wine

2 rosemary sprigs

1 garlic clove, peeled and crushed

1 rutabaga, peeled and cut into large dice

12 pearl onions, peeled

1 celery stalk, chopped

2 carrots, chopped

½ cup peas, fresh or thawed frozen

1 tbsp chopped flat-leaf parsley or minced chives

1. Trim the lamb shoulder of excess fat and gristle. Cut into 2-inch cubes and season with salt and pepper. Heat 2 tablespoons of the oil in a Dutch oven over high heat. Working in batches without crowding, sear the lamb pieces to a deep brown on all sides, about 8 minutes. Transfer the lamb to a bowl and set aside.

2. Add the remaining 2 tablespoons oil to the Dutch oven and heat over medium-high heat. Add the onion and cook, stirring occasionally, until golden, about 5 minutes. Add the tomato paste and cook, stirring frequently, until it darkens, about 1 minute.

3. Add the flour and cook, stirring frequently, to make a blond roux, about 5 minutes. Add the broth and wine to the pot, whisking well to work out any lumps. Return the lamb to the pot along with any juices released by the meat.

4. Bring to a gentle simmer over low to medium heat and add the rosemary sprigs and crushed garlic clove. Cover the pot and continue to stew over very low heat, stirring occasionally, until the lamb is cooked through, about 45 minutes.

5. Add the rutabaga, pearl onions, celery, and carrots; continue to stew until the lamb is tender and the vegetables are fully cooked, 30 to 35 minutes. Remove and discard the rosemary sprigs and garlic clove. Add the peas and simmer until all of the ingredients are heated through, 2 to 3 minutes. Season to taste with salt and pepper. Stir in the parsley or chives and serve the stew in heated bowls.

stewed lamb and chick peas

THIS DISH features flavors from the Mediterranean and combines a sofrito flavored with pancetta with a heady mix of spices including turmeric, coriander, and cumin.

MAKES 6 SERVINGS

2 tbsp olive oil

4 slices pancetta, minced

1 cup minced yellow onion

2 tsp minced garlic

½ tsp ground coriander

½ tsp ground cumin

Pinch ground turmeric

1½ lb boneless lamb leg meat, cut into 1-inch cubes

Salt as needed

Cracked white pepper as needed

1½ cups cooked or canned chick peas, drained

10 cups chicken broth or water, as needed

1½ cups diced carrot

1½ cups sliced leek, white and light-green parts

Zest of 1 orange

Zest of 1 lemon

1. Heat the oil in a casserole or Dutch oven over medium-high heat until it shimmers. Add the pancetta and sauté, stirring frequently, until the pancetta is translucent. Add the onion and garlic and sauté, stirring frequently, until translucent, 6 to 8 minutes Add the coriander, cumin, and turmeric and continue to sauté until aromatic, 1 to 2 minutes.

2. Season the lamb generously with salt and pepper and add it to the onion and garlic. Cook, stirring frequently, until the lamb has lost its raw look and is evenly coated with the onion-spice mixture, about 5 minutes. Add the chick peas to the pan, stir the mixture, and pour in enough broth or water to just cover the lamb and chick peas. Bring the mixture to a boil over high heat. Immediately reduce the heat and simmer gently over low heat, stirring occasionally, until the meat is nearly tender, 30 minutes.

3. Add the carrot, leek, and orange and lemon zest. Add more broth or water if necessary to keep the ingredients covered. Season to taste with salt and pepper.

4. Simmer until the lamb and the vegetables are very tender, 25 to 30 minutes. Serve in heated bowls.

green chile and pork stew with potatoes

*P*OBLANO CHILES and jalapeños give this dish its color and flavor. Whenever you work with hot chiles, wear gloves to protect your hands and be diligent about washing your hands, your tools, and the cutting board when you are done. Serve warm flour tortillas and a little grated Monterey Jack cheese to accompany this stew.

MAKES 6 SERVINGS

2 tbsp canola oil

2 lb boneless pork shoulder, cut into 1-inch cubes

Salt as needed

Freshly ground black pepper as needed

2 large yellow onions, cut into ¾-inch dice

1 tbsp minced garlic

6 cups chicken broth

¼ cup tomato purée

3 to 4 fresh poblano chiles, roasted, seeded, peeled, and cut into ½-inch pieces (page 9)

2 tbsp mild red chili powder

1 tbsp ground cumin

2 tsp ground Mexican oregano

2 fresh jalapeño peppers, seeded, finely minced

2 tbsp green Tabasco sauce

1 tsp white vinegar

3 cups cubed russet potatoes, peeled

2 cups cooked cannellini beans, rinsed and drained

⅓ cup chopped cilantro

3 tbsp chopped flat-leaf parsley

1. Heat the oil in a casserole or Dutch oven over medium heat until it shimmers. Season the pork with salt and pepper and sauté until lightly colored on all sides. Transfer the pork to a plate or dish using a slotted spoon, allowing most of the oil to drain back into the casserole. Return the casserole to the heat, add the onions and garlic and sauté, stirring frequently, until translucent, 6 to 8 minutes.

2. Return the pork and any juices it may have released to the casserole. Add the broth, tomato purée, poblanos, chili powder, cumin, and oregano; bring the liquid to a boil. Immediately adjust the heat for a gentle simmer. Simmer the stew, covered, for 1 hour, stirring occasionally.

3. Add the jalapeños, Tabasco, vinegar, potatoes, and beans. Continue to simmer, covered, until the potatoes and pork are very tender, about 20 minutes. Stir in the cilantro and parsley, and season to taste with additional salt and pepper.

4. Serve in heated bowls.

pork in a green curry sauce

*P*ALM SUGAR, also know as jaggery, is a coarse brown sugar made from the sap of the palmyra palm. It can be found in East Indian markets. In Mexican or South American markets, you may find it labeled as either *panela* or *piloncillo*.

MAKES 4 SERVINGS

Three 13.5-ounce cans coconut milk

½ cup Green Curry Paste (recipe follows)

2 lb boneless pork butt, cubed

6 wild lime leaves, bruised

¼ cup fish sauce

3 tbsp palm sugar

8 Thai eggplants, quartered

25 leaves Thai basil, left whole

2 Thai bird chiles, cut into thin strips

1. Skim the thick coconut cream from the top 1-inch of each can, reserving the remaining coconut milk. Place the cream in a casserole and cook, stirring constantly, until the coconut cream begins to separate, about 5 minutes. Add the curry paste and cook until aromatic, about 2 minutes.

2. Add the pork and lime leaves; mix well to coat the pork with the curry paste. Add the fish sauce, palm sugar, and reserved coconut milk; bring to a simmer over medium heat.

3. Add the eggplant and continue to simmer slowly, stirring occasionally, until cooked through, about 15 minutes. Add the basil leaves, then remove the curry from the heat, mix well, and transfer to a heated serving platter. Top with chile strips and serve at once.

Green Curry Paste

MAKES 1 CUP

1 tbsp coriander seeds

½ tsp cumin seeds

10 white peppercorns

3 shallots, thinly sliced

6 garlic cloves, thinly sliced

10 jalapeños, seeds removed

1 tbsp cilantro roots, finely chopped

2 tbsp lemongrass, thinly sliced

1 tsp galangal, ⅛-inch slices

1 tsp lime zest

3 wild lime leaves, chopped

2 tsp shrimp paste

1 tsp salt

1. Toast the coriander and cumin seeds in a small, dry skillet over medium-high heat. Transfer the seeds to a small bowl. Add the peppercorns to the hot skillet, roast in the same manner, and transfer to the same bowl.

2. Using a spice grinder, grind the roasted cumin, coriander, and peppercorns and set aside.

3. Place the remaining ingredients in a blender and grind into a fine paste. Transfer the paste to a bowl.

4. Stir the ground roasted spices into the paste until smooth. The curry paste is ready to use now or it can be refrigerated for up to 1 week.

pork adobo

ENJOYED THROUGHOUT the Philippines, adobo is a stew made of pork, poultry, fish, or even vegetables. The liberal use of vinegar gives it a unique flavor. In this recipe, we call for coconut palm vinegar; its mild, slightly sweet flavor gives the dish a traditional savor. If you can't locate it, you can substitute cider vinegar, white wine vinegar, or white balsamic vinegar. Steamed jasmine rice is a perfect accompaniment to this stew.

MAKES 8 SERVINGS

2 tsp annatto seeds

2 tbsp olive oil

3 lb pork butt, cut into 2-inch cubes

1 yellow onion, sliced thin

2 tbsp minced garlic

3 cups coconut palm vinegar

1¾ cups light soy sauce

1 tbsp cracked black peppercorns

12 bay leaves

¼ cup sugar

1. Soak the annatto seeds in ½ cup boiling water for 30 minutes. Strain the seeds and reserve the liquid. Discard the seeds.

2. Heat the olive oil in a Dutch oven or casserole over high heat. Add the pork (working in batches to avoid crowding the pan) and sear on all sides until brown, about 8 minutes. Remove from pot and set aside, discard any excess fat, leaving a small amount of oil in the bottom of the pot.

3. Return the Dutch oven or casserole to medium-high heat, add the onion, and sauté, stirring occasionally, until translucent, about 6 minutes. Add garlic and sauté, stirring constantly, until aromatic, about 30 seconds.

4. Return the pork and any juices it may have released to the pan along with the strained annatto liquid, vinegar, soy sauce, peppercorns, bay leaves, and sugar. Add enough additional water to cover the pork by ½ inch.

5. Bring the liquid to a boil. Immediately adjust the heat for a gentle simmer. Simmer the stew, covered, skimming any impurities that rise to the surface, until the pork is tender to the bite, about 45 minutes. Serve at once in heated bowls.

oxtail stew in red wine

Rabo de Toro

OXTAIL STEWS have incredible body and flavor. We recommend that you make this a day or two before you plan to eat it—the flavor deepens as it rests. Boiled, mashed, or pan-fried potatoes are good accompaniments to this dish, along with a glass of the wine you used to make the stew.

MAKES 6 SERVINGS

¼ cup olive oil

2¾ lb oxtail pieces

Salt as needed

Freshly ground black pepper as needed

2 cups chopped yellow onion

1½ cups chopped leek, white and light green portions

1 tsp minced garlic

½ cup diced plum tomato

1 tbsp sherry vinegar or as needed

1 tbsp honey

2 cups dry red wine, such as a good-quality Rioja

3 cups beef broth or as needed

4 parsley sprigs

4 thyme sprigs

1 bay leaf

2 tbsp chopped parsley, for garnish

1. Heat the oil in a casserole or Dutch oven over high heat until it shimmers. Season the oxtail pieces generously with salt and pepper; add in a single layer to the hot oil. (Work in batches if necessary to avoid crowding the pieces.) Sauté the oxtail, turning as necessary, until browned on all sides, about 10 minutes. Transfer to a plate, letting the oil drain back into the casserole. Cover the oxtail loosely and set aside.

2. Return the casserole to high heat until the oil shimmers. Add the onion, leek, and garlic and sauté, stirring occasionally, until golden brown, about 15 minutes. Add the diced tomato and cook until it deepens in color and smells sweet, about 2 minutes.

3. Add 1 tbsp sherry vinegar and the honey and stir until the honey is dissolved. Return the oxtail pieces and any juices they may have released to the casserole and fold the oxtail into the vegetables gently with a wooden spoon.

4. Add the red wine and enough of the broth to cover the oxtail. Bring to a simmer over low heat. Tie the parsley, thyme, and bay leaf together into a bouquet garni and add to the stew. Cover the casserole and simmer very gently over low heat until the meat on the oxtail is nearly falling from the bone, 2 to 3 hours.

5. Transfer the oxtail pieces to a heated serving bowl and keep warm. Remove and discard the bouquet garni. Return the casserole to the heat. Skim the fat and oil from the surface and bring to a simmer over medium-high heat. Simmer rapidly until the sauce thickens slightly, about 5 minutes. Season to taste with additional sherry vinegar, salt, and pepper. Pour the sauce over the oxtail pieces, garnish with parsley, and serve at once.

beef stew with onions and cheese
Stifado

THERE ARE plenty of variations on this Greek stew. Some cooks include walnuts and dried currants, while others add a few additional vegetables such as turnips, parsnips, carrots, or potatoes to round out the stew. Red wine is a good match for the bold flavors in this stew, but white wine is an equally appropriate choice.

MAKE 6 TO 8 SERVINGS

3 tbsp butter

3 lb boneless beef top round, cut into 1½-inch cubes

1 tsp salt

¼ tsp freshly ground black pepper

2 tsp minced garlic

1 bay leaf

1 cinnamon stick, 2 inches

½ cup dry red wine

3 tbsp red wine vinegar

1 cup tomato sauce (see page 165)

1 tsp sugar

24 pearl onions

1 cup feta cheese, crumbled

1. Preheat the oven to 325 degrees F.

2. Heat the butter in a casserole or Dutch oven over medium-high heat. Season the beef with salt and pepper and add to the hot butter. Sauté, stirring occasionally, until the beef is no longer red. Add the garlic, bay leaf, and cinnamon. Cover tightly and cook over low heat for 10 minutes.

3. Add the wine and vinegar. Cover tightly and place in the preheated oven. Continue to stew in the oven until the meat is nearly tender, about 1 hour.

4. Add the tomato sauce, sugar, and pearl onions to the stew; stir to combine. Return to the oven and continue to stew until the meat is very tender, about 1 hour.

5. Five minutes before serving, remove and discard the bay leaf and cinnamon stick and stir in the crumbled cheese. Serve hot in heated bowls.

catalan beef stew

with Orange Peel and Black Olives (Estofado de Catalan)

THE CUISINE of Spain is rapidly becoming more familiar to cooks and restaurant-goers. This typical dish marries a flavorful cut of beef from the shoulder with some typical Catalonian ingredients. Bitter oranges are traditional, but if you don't have access to a bitter orange, use a Valencia (juice) orange and a touch of lime juice for nearly the same flavor profile.

MAKES 4 SERVINGS

1 tbsp olive oil

5 slices bacon, thick-cut, diced

2 lb boneless beef chuck or bottom round, cut into 2-inch pieces

Salt as needed

Freshly ground black pepper as needed

2 cups chopped yellow onion

2 cups red wine

2 tbsp orange peel julienne

2 bay leaves

2 tsp minced garlic

2 parsley sprigs, minced

1 cup Spanish black olives, pitted

1. Heat the oil in a casserole or Dutch oven over medium-high heat until it shimmers. Add the bacon, and sauté until the bacon is crisped and browned, 5 minutes. Transfer the bacon to a bowl with a slotted spoon, letting the oil drain back into the casserole.

2. Return the casserole to the heat and heat the oil until it shimmers. Season the beef generously with salt and pepper. Add the beef (working in batches to avoid crowding the pan) and sear on all sides until brown, about 8 minutes. Transfer the beef to the bowl with the bacon using a slotted spoon, letting the oil drain back into the casserole. Add the onion and sauté, stirring occasionally, until deeply caramelized, 25 to 30 minutes.

3. Return the beef and bacon to the casserole, add the red wine, orange peel, bay leaves, garlic, and parsley; bring the liquid to a boil. Immediately adjust the heat for a gentle simmer. Season the stew to taste with salt and pepper throughout cooking time. Simmer the stew, covered, until the beef is nearly tender, about 2 hours. Add the olives and continue to simmer until the beef is fork tender, 1 to 1½ hours. Serve in heated bowls.

PITTING OLIVES

You don't have to take the pits out of your olives, but it does make eating the stew a little easier. You can buy cherry and olive pitters at most stores that carry cookware appliances or gadgets. If you don't have a pitter, though, you can either cut the olive away from the pit using a sharp paring knife, or you can fish the pit out of the olive using a paper clip. Open the paper clip out so that you have hooks. Insert the rounded end of one of the hooks into the olive and catch the pit in the bend of your hook and pull out the pit.

CARTOUCHE

To be sure that this dish is as moist and succulent as possible, use this tip: Cut a piece of cooking parchment that will fit snugly inside your casserole or Dutch oven. Once the stew is simmering very slowly, carefully push the paper down onto the surface of the stew to keep the meat completely submerged. Professional chefs refer to this paper lid as a cartouche.

meat and potatoes

Nikujaga

bEEF AND potatoes are simmered together with onions in a sauce flavored with mirin and soy. Use the water from holding the cut potatoes as part of the stew. The starch from the potatoes will thicken it slightly.

MAKES 4 SERVINGS

4 medium russet or Idaho potatoes

2 tbsp peanut or sesame oil

3 yellow onions, sliced ¼-inch thick

1½ lb boneless beef sirloin, sliced ¼-inch thick

½ cup soy sauce

3 tbsp mirin

3 tbsp sugar

1. Peel the potatoes, cut them into 1-inch cubes, and hold them in a bowl, covered with cold water. (Reserve the water in which the potatoes are held; it will become part of the stew.)

2. Heat the oil in a casserole or Dutch oven over high heat until it shimmers. Add the onions and sauté until translucent, 6 to 8 minutes. Add the beef and cook, stirring frequently, until no longer pink on the outside, about 4 minutes.

3. Add the soy sauce, mirin, and sugar; stir to coat the ingredients evenly and bring to a gentle simmer over low heat.

4. Add the potatoes to the beef and fold them gently into the mixture. Spread the potatoes and beef into an even layer and then add enough of the potato water to just cover the ingredients. Bring the stew to a gentle simmer, cover, and simmer until the beef is cooked, 5 to 6 minutes. Remove the cover and continue to simmer until the potatoes are tender and the sauce is lightly thickened, 5 to 6 minutes. Serve in heated bowls.

saigon beef stew

with Lemongrass and Anise

SLICE THE onion and carrots paper-thin for this dish. Cutting the carrots on the diagonal gives them a pleasing shape. You can make plain round slices into flowers by cutting three or four evenly-spaced grooves into the carrot with a paring knife before you slice it.

MAKES 6 SERVINGS

3 tbsp annatto oil

2 tbsp chopped shallots

2 tsp minced garlic

1 tbsp curry powder

2 tsp minced Thai bird chiles or as needed

½ tsp ground anise

Salt as needed

Freshly ground black paper as needed

1½ lb beef chuck roast, cut into 1½-inch cubes

3 cups beef or chicken broth

3 lemongrass stalks, crushed and cut into 3-inch pieces

2 tbsp fish sauce or as needed

1 tbsp soy sauce or as needed

1 tbsp sugar

2 cups thinly sliced carrots, cut on the diagonal

1 cup thinly sliced yellow onion

½ cup loosely packed Thai basil leaves, torn into pieces

½ cup loosely packed cilantro leaves, torn into pieces

1. Heat the annatto oil in a casserole or Dutch oven over high heat until it shimmers. Add the shallots and garlic and stir until fragrant, about 30 seconds. Add the curry powder, chiles, anise, and a pinch of salt and pepper. Sauté, stirring frequently, until aromatic, about 1 minute. Spoon half of this shallot-spice mixture into a bowl and set aside

2. Add the beef to the casserole and stir until evenly blended with the remaining shallot-spice mixture. Sauté until the beef has lost its raw look, about 5 minutes. Add the broth, lemongrass, fish sauce, soy sauce, and sugar and bring to a boil over high heat. Immediately reduce the heat until the stew is simmering gently. Continue to simmer, skimming occasionally, until the beef is nearly tender, about 15 minutes. Add the carrots and onion and simmer until the beef and carrots are tender, about 15 minutes.

3. Stir in the reserved shallot-spice mixture. Season to taste with salt, pepper, and additional fish sauce or soy sauce. Serve in heated soup plates garnished with basil and cilantro leaves.

ANNATTO OIL

Brightly colored, aromatic annatto oil makes this dish unusual. If you can't find annatto oil, make your own: Heat 1 cup canola oil in a small saucepan. When it is shimmering, add 5 tablespoons annatto seeds. The seeds will foam up and sputter. Immediately pull the pan off the heat, let the seeds steep for 10 minutes, and then strain out and discard the seeds.

veal stew with polenta

tHIS DISH is a variation on a shepherd's pie, with polenta to replace the potato topping and a vegetable-laden stew that features tender veal. If possible, buy a boneless shoulder (or arm) or the bottom round and cut it into pieces yourself.

MAKES 6 SERVINGS

3 lb boneless veal stew meat, cut into 1-inch cubes

Salt as needed

Freshly ground black pepper as needed

All-purpose flour for dusting as needed

2 tbsp olive oil, or as needed

¾ cup minced onion

1 cup large-dice carrot

1 cup large-dice celery root (celeriac)

2 tbsp tomato paste

1½ cups dry red wine

6 cups beef broth, or as needed

2 sprigs rosemary

2 sprigs thyme

1 bay leaf

1½ cups Brussels sprouts, trimmed and halved

1 cup pearl onions, peeled and blanched

1 cup green beans, blanched

3 cups cooked polenta (see note)

1. Season the veal generously with salt and pepper. Pour some flour into a shallow plate and dust the veal pieces in the flour.

2. Heat the oil in a Dutch oven or casserole over medium-high heat until it shimmers. Sauté the veal in the oil, stirring frequently, until the veal is a light golden color on all sides, 8 to 10 minutes. Transfer the veal to a pan and keep warm.

3. Return the pan to the heat. Add the onion, carrot, and celery root. Sauté, stirring frequently, until the onion is lightly browned, 8 to 10 minutes. Add the tomato paste and continue to sauté until there is a sweet aroma and the tomato paste darkens in color, about 5 minutes. Add the wine and stir well to dissolve all of the drippings. Return the veal and any juices it may have released to the casserole. Add enough broth to cover the veal by about 1 inch. Bring the broth to a boil, add the rosemary, thyme, and bay leaf, and reduce the heat to low. Simmer, covered, stirring occasionally, until the veal is almost tender, about 45 minutes. Season to taste with additional salt and pepper as the stew simmers. Remove the herbs and discard.

4. Add the Brussels sprouts and pearl onions to the stew. Simmer, covered, until the vegetables are nearly tender, about 20 minutes. Add the green beans and simmer until they are very hot, another 5 minutes. Season to taste with additional salt and pepper.

5. Preheat the oven to 375 degrees F.

6. Transfer the stew to a casserole dish or baking dish. Top with an even layer of the polenta. Bake until the stew and polenta are very hot and the crust is lightly browned, about 20 minutes. Divide the stew evenly among heated bowls and serve.

MAKING POLENTA

Soft polenta, fresh from the pot, makes a perfect topping for this stew or as a side dish to serve along with braised dishes or stews. You can add fresh herbs, butter, or cheese to the polenta while it is still hot for a little additional flavor.

To make 6 servings of polenta, bring 3½ cups chicken broth or water to a rolling boil. Add about 1 teaspoon of salt, or to taste. Measure out 1 cup of coarse yellow cornmeal and add it very gradually while you are stirring constantly. Some cooks add the cornmeal just a pinch at a time so they won't end up with lumps. Simmer over low heat and stir the polenta frequently. It will thicken and start to pull away from the sides of the pot. Polenta usually takes at least 35 to 40 minutes to develop a creamy texture and a robust flavor.

fava bean stew

*I*F YOU can find fresh fava beans, buy about 3 pounds of beans and shell them to make about 3 cups of beans. Fresh fava beans don't require soaking and the dish will finish cooking in about 30 minutes instead of 2 hours.

MAKES 4 SERVINGS

2 cups dry fava beans

Cold water, as needed

2 tbsp olive oil

1 medium yellow onion, quartered

1 tsp minced garlic

4 oz morcilla (blood sausage), sliced in to ¼-inch-thick slices

6 oz chorizo, sliced in to ¼-inch-thick slices

4 oz slab bacon, sliced in to ¼-inch-thick slices

1 pinch saffron threads, lightly crushed

Salt as needed

Freshly ground black pepper as needed

¼ cup chopped parsley

1. Soak the beans in enough cold water to cover for at least 24 and up to 36 hours.

2. Heat the oil in a casserole or Dutch oven over medium-high heat until it shimmers. Add the onion and garlic and sauté, stirring occasionally, until the onion is browned, about 10 minutes. Add the morcilla, chorizo, and slab bacon and sauté in the hot oil until browned, 6 to 8 minutes

3. Add the drained soaked beans to the casserole and add enough cold water to cover them by about 2 inches. Bring the water to a boil over high heat. Immediately reduce the heat to establish a gentle simmer. Add the saffron and season to taste with salt and pepper. Simmer, covered, until the beans are tender, about 2 hours. Adjust the consistency with cold water if it is getting too thick.

4. Season to taste with salt and pepper. Garnish with chopped parsley and serve in warm bowls.

chicken clay pot

Cooking in clay pots is a big part of some Chinese cuisines. The unglazed cooker can go from the oven to the table, and it retains heat to keep foods hot at the table. To learn more about clay pots, see the note below.

MAKES 4 SERVINGS

1¼ lb boneless skinless chicken breast

Salt as needed

Freshly ground black pepper as needed

⅔ cup water

½ cup fish sauce

⅓ cup tightly packed brown sugar

1 tbsp canola oil

6 sprigs fresh cilantro, chopped (including roots and stems)

2 Thai bird chiles, chopped

1 tsp garlic, minced

1 tsp minced ginger root

1 tsp lime juice

1 tsp red wine vinegar

2 tbsp chopped cilantro leaves

1. Preheat the oven to 425 degrees F if you are not using a clay pot cooker.

2. Cut the chicken into ½-inch cubes. Season well with salt and pepper.

3. Stir together the water, fish sauce, brown sugar, oil, cilantro, Thai bird chiles, garlic, ginger, lime juice, and vinegar in a small bowl until the sugar is completely dissolved.

4. Put the chicken in a soaked clay pot (see note for pot preparation) or an ovenproof casserole with a lid. Pour the fish sauce mixture over the chicken pieces.

5. Put the clay pot into a cold oven and set the temperature for 400 degrees F. (If you are using an ovenproof casserole, put it into a preheated oven.) Cook in the oven until the chicken is cooked through and the liquid has thickened and coats the chicken, 12 to 15 minutes. Garnish with cilantro and serve immediately directly from the clay pot or casserole.

CLAY POTS

Clay is an ancient cooking medium. You may have even seen some contemporary recipes that call for foods to be wrapped in wet clay and then roasted or baked. Clay pots give foods a distinctive flavor, but they require careful handling.

Be sure to buy your clay pot from a reputable source. Some unglazed clay cooking equipment may contain harmful or toxic substances. Before you use a clay pot for the first time, let it soak in cold water overnight. The next day, let it air dry. After that, you will only need to soak the pot for 15 minutes before starting to prepare a dish.

Once you've added all of your ingredients to the pot, place the covered clay pot into the center of a cold oven. As the oven heats up, it will gradually bring the pot up to the desired temperature. If you put a cold clay pot into a hot oven, you risk cracking the pot. Most clay pot recipes call for a temperature of at least 400°F.

Never place a hot pot on a cold or wet surface. It will surely crack. Use a hot pad or wooden cutting board. Some clay cookers are flameproof for use on a stovetop or even a grill, but be sure that your clay pot can handle direct heat.

To clean your clay pot, rinse it out with very hot water and use a stiff brush to scrub the pot clean. Don't use soap and never put a clay pot in the dishwasher. If there are stains or if your clay pot has absorbed odors, let the cooker soak overnight filled with a mixture of water and ¼ cup of baking soda.

shrimp and chicken jambalaya

aNDOUILLE SAUSAGE is an important part of this jambalaya because it adds a rich, smoky flavor along with plenty of garlic and spice. If Andouille sausage isn't easy to find in your area, substitute other available spicy sausages such as chorizo or linguiça.

MAKES 8 SERVINGS

3 tbsp canola oil

1½ lb chicken, thigh meat, cubed

Salt as needed

Freshly ground black pepper as needed

1 lb andouille sausage, sliced ½-inch thick

2 cups minced yellow onion

2 cups diced green bell pepper

1½ cups diced celery

2 tsp minced garlic

2 tbsp paprika

¼ tsp ground cayenne

¼ tsp ground white pepper

2 cups chopped plum tomatoes, peeled and seeded, juice reserved

3 cups chicken broth or as needed

1 bay leaf

¼ cup basil chiffonade

2 tsp chopped fresh thyme

1 tsp Tabasco

30 shrimp, 21 to 25 count, peeled and deveined

4 cups cooked short-grain rice

1 cup sliced scallions, white and green portions

1. Heat the oil in a Dutch oven over high heat until it shimmers. Season the chicken with salt and pepper and then sear in the hot oil, turning as necessary, until golden on all sides, about 8 minutes. Transfer to a warm plate or pan. Add the sausage to the pan and continue to sauté until it is lightly browned on both sides, about 6 minutes. Transfer to the same plate or pan as the chicken and reserve.

2. Add the onion, bell pepper, celery, garlic, paprika, cayenne, and white pepper to the Dutch oven; cook over medium-low heat, stirring frequently, until the vegetables start to release some of their juices and are beginning to soften, about 10 minutes. Add the tomatoes with their juices and simmer briefly. Add the broth and bay leaf and bring the jambalaya to a simmer. Cover the Dutch oven and simmer, stirring occasionally, until the vegetables are almost completely tender, 15 minutes.

3. Return the browned chicken and sausage to the Dutch oven, along with any juices they may have released. Add the basil, thyme, and Tabasco, and return to a simmer over low heat until flavorful, about 10 minutes. Add the shrimp to the jambalaya and simmer until the shrimp are cooked all the way through, 5 minutes.

4. Add the cooked rice and mix well. Serve the jambalaya in heated bowls, topped with the scallions.

chicken and prawn ragout

Mar i Muntanya

PRAWNS ARE a distinct species, differing from shrimp in their gill structure, but in the United States, the term *prawn* typically refers to a very large shrimp. In England and Australia, the term *prawn* is used instead of shrimp, no matter what the size. For this recipe, select large or even jumbo shrimp and leave the shells on the shrimp. The shells contribute a lot of flavor.

MAKES 6 SERVINGS

6 chicken thighs

Salt as needed

Freshly ground black pepper as needed

3 tbsp olive oil

1½ lb shrimp (16 to 20 count), in the shell

2 cups chopped yellow onion

1½ cups chopped plum tomatoes (fresh or canned)

¾ cup dry white wine

8 cups chicken broth, as needed

Pernod as needed

½ cup Picada (recipe follows)

1. Season the chicken thighs with salt and pepper.

2. Heat the oil in a casserole or Dutch oven over high heat until it shimmers. Add the chicken pieces and sauté, turning as necessary, until golden brown on all sides, about 10 minutes. Transfer the chicken pieces to a bowl using a slotted spoon, letting the oil drain back into the casserole.

3. Return the casserole to the heat and heat the oil until it shimmers. Add the shrimp and sauté until the shells are a bright pink or red, about 4 minutes. Transfer the shrimp to a separate bowl using a slotted spoon, letting the oil drain back into the casserole.

4. Add the onion to the casserole and sauté, stirring occasionally, until deep brown, about 20 minutes. Add the tomatoes and simmer, stirring occasionally, until very thick, about 15 minutes.

5. Add the wine to the casserole and stir well to dissolve any drippings. Bring the wine to a simmer and cook until the wine reduces by ½. Add the chicken pieces and any juices they may have released to the casserole. Pour in enough broth to cover the chicken by 1 inch. Simmer, uncovered, over medium-low heat until the chicken is nearly cooked through, about 20 minutes.

6. Add the Pernod and continue to simmer until the chicken is completely cooked, about 10 minutes. Add the shrimp and simmer until they are heated through, 2 to 3 minutes. Season to taste with salt and pepper. Add the picada and simmer until the ragout is flavorful and lightly thickened, 2 minutes. Serve in heated bowls.

Picada

MAKES ½ CUP

3 baguette slices, about ½ inch thick

2 tbsp minced garlic

24 almonds, blanched and roasted

2 tbsp chopped flat-leaf parsley

2 tbsp extra-virgin olive oil, or as needed

Crush or grind the baguette slices, garlic, and almonds in a food processor, blender, or mortar and pestle until smooth. Add the parsley and blend it into the mixture. Stir in enough oil to make thick paste.

dried salt cod, mexican style

Bacalao a la Mexicana

bASED UPON salt cod, or *bacalao*, and traditionally served at Mexican Christmas celebrations, this stew is made with a rich *mole* and finished with almonds. The usual accompaniment is toasted tortillas. To learn more about buying and preparing salt cod, see the note below.

MAKE 8 SERVINGS

2 lb dried salt cod

2 ancho chiles, toasted

4 cups diced plum tomatoes

½ cup olive oil

2 cups diced yellow onion

2 tbsp minced garlic

1 bay leaf

1 tsp ground cinnamon

1 tsp freshly ground black pepper

3 red bell peppers, roasted, peeled and diced

½ cup sliced almonds

¼ cup raisins

½ cup stuffed green olives

2 tbsp capers

2 tbsp chopped parsley

2½ cups diced cooked potatoes

1. Soak the cod in cold water for 12 hours, changing the water every 3 or 4 hours. Drain. Place the cod in a saucepan, add enough cold water to cover, and bring to a boil. Drain the cod, letting it cool until it is easy to handle, and then pull the cod apart into shreds; set aside.

2. Remove the stems and seeds from the ancho chiles and soak them in hot water for 10 minutes. Drain the chiles and purée with the tomatoes in a blender until smooth. Strain the mixture and set aside.

3. Heat the oil in a large skillet over medium heat until it shimmers. Add the onion and garlic and sauté until transparent, 6 to 8 minutes. Add the chile/tomato purée and cook over low heat, stirring occasionally, until the mixture thickens, 5 to 6 minutes. Add the cod, bay leaf, cinnamon, black pepper, bell peppers, almonds, raisins, olives, capers, and parsley. Cook over medium heat for 10 minutes, stirring occasionally. Add the potatoes, cover, and cook until heated through, about 12 minutes. Serve at once.

SALT COD

Known as baccala in Italian, bacalao in Spanish, bacalhau in Portuguese, morue in French, and salt cod in English, this heavily salted fish is typically sold in Italian, Greek or Portuguese markets and at some larger grocery chains. When buying salt cod, look for uniform texture and color; avoid pieces with a yellowish tint. The flesh should be pliable and compact, not woody. Look for pieces that have a uniform thickness; they will soak evenly. Skinless and boneless salt cod is easier to handle.

Cooks disagree on the appropriate length of time to soak salt cod. Some suggest 8 hours while others soak the fish for up to 3 days. We feel that 12 hours is just enough time to remove the overpowering saltiness. Cut the cod fillets into chunks and put them into a large bowl. Add enough cold water to completely cover the fish and put the bowl in the refrigerator. Replace the water every 3 or 4 hours. After the fillets have been soaked and drained, the fish should feel soft and pliable, with only a hint of brininess. If your salt cod still has the skin and bones, pull off the skin, pick out the bones, and break the fish into flakes.

seafood with coconut water

Mariscos con Agua de Coco

C HOOSE A casserole or other flameproof dish that is wider than it is tall for this quick-cooking seafood stew.

MAKES 8 SERVINGS

3 tbsp canola oil

1 cup Salsa Verde de Tampico (recipe follows)

1 cup mint leaves, stems removed, loosely packed, chopped after measuring

½ lb sea scallops

¼ lb shrimp, peeled and deveined

6 oz salmon fillet, skinned, cut into 1-inch cubes

Salt as needed

Freshly ground black pepper as needed

1 cup coconut water (see note)

½ cup seafood or vegetable broth

1. Heat the oil in a casserole or Dutch oven over high heat until it shimmers. Add the salsa and chopped mint and cook, stirring often, until heated through, about 2 minutes.

2. Season the scallops, shrimp, and cubed salmon with salt and pepper. Add them to the casserole and stir to coat evenly.

3. Add the coconut water and broth and bring to a simmer over medium heat. Simmer slowly, uncovered, until the seafood is cooked through and opaque, 2 to 3 minutes. Serve in heated bowls.

COCONUT WATER

Buying a fresh coconut can be a challenge. When you find them in the market, look for coconuts with a dry shell and no signs of mold, especially around the eyes. Shake the coconut and listen for a sloshing sound that indicates plenty of coconut water inside. You can substitute equal parts coconut milk and water instead.

To drain the liquid from a fresh coconut, use an ice pick or corkscrew to pierce two of the coconut's eyes. Set a strainer over a glass measuring pitcher and line it with a coffee filter. Pour the liquid from the coconut into the strainer. If you don't have quite the amount of coconut water called for in the recipe, supplement the coconut water with cold water.

Salsa Verde de Tampico

MAKES ABOUT 1½ CUPS

6 fresh jalapeño or serrano chiles, stems removed, halved crosswise

1 medium yellow onion, quartered

5 garlic cloves, coarsely chopped

¼ cup canola or olive oil

½ cup loosely packed cilantro leaves

1 tsp dried Mexican oregano, crumbled

Place all the ingredients in a blender or food processor and pulse until chopped to a slightly coarse consistency.

tuna and potato stew

Marmitako

*Y*OU MAY have thought that all really good stews have a stock or broth as a major ingredient. In this stew, we recommend using water, rather than broth or stock, which might mask the sweet, earthy flavors of these ingredients.

MAKES 6 SERVINGS

2 tbsp olive oil

1 cup chopped yellow onion

3 Anaheim chiles, diced

6 garlic cloves, thinly sliced

1 bay leaf

1 cup dry white wine

4 cups water

6 to 8 saffron threads, lightly crushed

2 ancho chiles

3 cups medium-dice Yukon Gold potatoes

2 lb tuna, cut into 1-inch cubes

Salt as needed

Freshly ground black pepper as needed

2 tbsp chopped flat-leaf parsley

1. Heat the oil in a casserole or Dutch oven over high heat until it shimmers. Add the onion and chiles and sauté, stirring frequently, until softened and translucent, about 10 minutes.

2. Add the garlic, bay leaf, and wine. Simmer rapidly until the wine reduces by half. Add the water, saffron, and ancho chiles, and bring to a boil over high heat. Add the potatoes, reduce the heat to medium and simmer, covered, until the potatoes are nearly tender, about 20 minutes.

3. Season the tuna cubes with salt and add to the stew. Simmer slowly until the tuna is cooked through and the potatoes are very tender, 5 to 6 minutes. Season to taste with salt and pepper. Serve in heated bowls garnished with chopped parsley.

lamb meatballs stewed with hot tomatoes

Kefta

FRAGRANT AND flavorful meatballs like these are a staple in many Mediterranean cuisines. Be sure to keep the ingredients for the meatballs very cold until you are ready to mix them. It helps the meatballs hold together as they simmer.

MAKES 6 SERVINGS

MEATBALLS

1 lb ground lamb or beef

½ cup coarsely grated yellow onion

¼ cup dry bread crumbs

¼ cup chopped flat-leaf parsley

1 tsp minced garlic

¾ tsp ground cumin

¾ tsp paprika

½ tsp minced ginger root

¼ tsp ground cardamom

3 tbsp water

¼ chopped cilantro

1 tsp salt or as needed

¼ tsp ground black pepper or as needed

2 tbsp olive oil

½ cup chopped yellow onion

¼ tsp harissa (page 143)

¼ tsp cumin

¼ tsp cinnamon

2 or 3 saffron threads, lightly crushed, optional

3 cups Tomato Sauce (page 165)

1. Combine the lamb or beef, grated onion, bread crumbs, parsley, garlic, cumin, paprika, ginger root, cardamom, water, 2 tablespoons cilantro, 1 teaspoon salt, and ¼ teaspoon pepper in a bowl. Mix by hand with a wooden spoon until slightly sticky. Chill at least 1 and up to 8 hours before shaping into oval meatballs about 1 inch in diameter.

2. Heat the olive oil in a deep skillet or Dutch oven over medium-high heat until it shimmers. Add the meatballs to the oil and cook, turning as necessary, until they are browned on all sides, about 8 minutes. Transfer the meatballs to a plate and set aside.

3. Add the chopped onion, harissa, cumin, cinnamon, and saffron, if using, to the pan. Sauté, stirring frequently, until the onion is tender and translucent, 6 to 8 minutes. Add the tomato sauce to the pan, stirring well to dissolve any browned bits in the pan. Bring the sauce to a simmer. Return the meatballs to the sauce along with any juices they may have released. Simmer the meatballs over low heat until they are cooked through and the sauce is very flavorful, about 15 minutes. Stir in the remaining cilantro and season to taste with salt and pepper. Serve at once on heated plates.

monkfish stew

with Wine, Peppers, and Almonds

For an elegant presentation, you can puree the vegetables and broth before you add the ground almonds. This recipe is for a chunky, rustic stew with lots of textures and colors. A flameproof earthenware casserole, or *cazuela*, is perfect for this dish, but be certain that any earthenware cookware is manufactured to stand up to direct heat.

MAKES 6 SERVINGS

⅓ cup olive oil

2½ lb monkfish fillets, cut into 2-inch cubes

Salt as needed

Freshly ground black pepper as needed

2 cups sliced yellow onion

1½ cups thinly sliced carrots

2 tsp thinly sliced garlic

2 cups diced plum tomatoes

2 tbsp all-purpose flour

2½ cups fish or vegetable broth

⅔ cup dry white wine

1 bay leaf

⅓ cup blanched almonds, whole

8 to 10 saffron threads, lightly crushed

1⅓ cups green peas, blanched if fresh or thawed if frozen

1 cup roasted red bell pepper strips

1. Heat half of the olive oil in a casserole or *cazuela* over medium-high heat until it shimmers. Season the monkfish with salt and pepper. Sauté in the hot oil until colored on both sides, 3 to 4 minutes. Work in batches to avoid overcrowding the pan. Transfer to a plate or dish with a slotted spoon letting the oil drain back into the casserole.

2. Return the casserole to the stove and heat the remaining oil until it shimmers. Add the onion, carrots, and 1 tsp garlic and sauté, stirring occasionally, until translucent, about 6 minutes. Add the tomatoes and cook until tender and broken down, then add the flour. Stir well to blend the flour in evenly and cook until pasty, about 5 minutes.

3. Stir in the broth and wine until evenly blended. Use a whisk if necessary to work out any lumps in the stew. Add the bay leaf and bring the mixture to a boil. Immediately reduce the heat until the mixture simmers slowly. Simmer, stirring frequently, until thickened and flavorful, 10 to 12 minutes.

4. Pound the almonds, saffron, and the remaining garlic in a mortar and pestle or chop them together with a chef's knife to a coarse paste. Add the paste to the tomato and broth mixture, stir well, and simmer 2 to 3 minutes.

5. Arrange the monkfish on top of the stew and top with the peas and roasted peppers. Season to taste with salt and pepper. Cover tightly and simmer until the fish is opaque throughout, 10 to 12 minutes. Serve in heated bowls.

vegetable stew

tHIS HEARTY and warming stew can be doubled and left-overs will freeze well. Cool the stew to room temperature, store in an airtight container, and freeze for up to 2 weeks. Thaw in the refrigerator or microwave. Serve the stew over a bed of couscous or noodles.

MAKES 4 SERVINGS

1½ tsp ginger root, minced

½ tsp paprika

¼ tsp ground cumin

¼ tsp turmeric

¼ tsp dry mustard

¼ tsp ground coriander

¼ tsp ground cinnamon

¼ tsp ground cardamom

⅛ tsp cayenne

1 tbsp olive oil

1 large yellow onion, diced

1 medium leek, cleaned and sliced thin

2 tsp minced garlic

½ cup diced pumpkin

½ cup diced butternut squash

½ cup diced zucchini

3 cups low-sodium vegetable broth

1½ cups diced eggplant

2 carrots, diced

1 celery stalk, diced

⅓ cup currants

3 tbsp tomato puree

⅓ cup cooked or canned chick peas, rinsed

⅓ cup cooked fava beans

2 tsp fresh lemon juice

¼ tsp salt

1½ tsp grated lemon zest

1. Combine the ginger, paprika, cumin, turmeric, mustard, coriander, cinnamon, cardamom, and cayenne. Toast the spice blend in a dry, nonstick skillet over low heat, until the blend is fragrant, about 2 minutes.

2. Heat the oil in a in a large pot over medium-high heat until it shimmers. Add the onion, leek, and garlic; sauté, stirring frequently, until translucent, about 3 to 5 minutes. Add the spice blend and sauté until fragrant, about 30 seconds. Stir in the pumpkin, squash, and zucchini. Add enough broth to cover the vegetables; simmer 10 minutes. Add the remaining broth, the eggplant, carrots, celery, currants, and tomato puree. Simmer until the vegetables are tender, about 25 minutes.

3. Stir the chick peas and fava beans into the simmering vegetables; add the lemon juice and salt. Cover the pot and cook until heated through. Divide the stew among 4 bowls and sprinkle with the grated lemon zest.

stewed ginseng game hens

*I*F YOU can only find game hens that are more than one pound, you may want to divide larger hens in half before serving. To make this dish easier to eat, you can cut the breast meat away from the rib cage, pulling the hen away from the bones as you work, the same way you might pull off a tight-fitting glove. Kimchi is a Korean pickled cabbage condiment that can be found in many Asian markets.

MAKES 4 SERVINGS

1½ cups medium-grain white rice

4 Cornish game hens

Salt as needed

Freshly ground black pepper as needed

5 garlic cloves, peeled and left whole

20 jujube (Chinese or Indian dates)

2 ginseng root, whole, washed, peel on

4 scallions, minced

1 cup kimchi, optional

1. Rinse the rice in cool water until the water runs clear. Place the rice in a bowl with enough cold water to cover, and soak for 30 minutes

2. Remove the giblets and neck from the hens (reserve to make broth or stock if desired). Rinse and dry hens and then season generously with salt and pepper inside and out.

3. Spoon the soaked rice into the cavities of the hens, dividing it equally among them, and truss to close the openings.

4. Place the hens, garlic, dates, and ginseng in a large pot. Add enough cold water to cover the hens. Bring the water to a boil over high heat. Reduce the heat to low and simmer slowly, partially covered, skimming as necessary, until the hens are cooked through, the rice is tender, and liquid reduces by about half, about 45 minutes.

5. Serve whole hens in a large bowl garnished with scallions and accompanied by kimchi.

summer stew au pistou

SERVE THIS quick-cooking vegetable stew with a hearty red wine to stand up to the bold flavors of the pancetta and *pistou*, a mixture of tomatoes, basil, and garlic that is beloved in some parts of France as a final flavoring for soups and stews. Letting the stew rest briefly before serving gives the pistou's flavors a chance to open up.

MAKES 4 SERVINGS

4 cups water, or as needed

2 slices pancetta

1 large carrot, cut into medium dice

1 Idaho potato, cut into medium dice

3 small yellow onions, cut into medium dice

1 cup cooked or canned cannelini beans, drained

1 cup green beans

1 cup medium-dice zucchini

2 scallions, green and white portions, cut into ⅓-inch lengths

¾ cup small dried pasta (shells, bow ties, or orrechietti)

Salt as needed

Freshly ground black pepper as needed

½ cup diced plum tomatoes

⅓ cup chopped basil

2 tsp minced garlic

1 tbsp extra-virgin olive oil

1. Combine the water and pancetta in a large soup pot. Bring to a boil, reduce heat to a low simmer, and add the carrot, potato, onions, and cannelini beans. Simmer slowly over low heat until the potatoes are tender, 30 to 35 minutes. Add the greens beans, zucchini, scallions, and pasta; simmer until all the vegetables are flavorful and the pasta is tender, 20 to 25 minutes. Season to taste with salt and pepper.

2. While the stew cooks, make the pistou: Chop together the tomatoes, basil, and garlic with a chef's knife or in a food processor to make a relatively smooth paste. Transfer to a bowl and stir in the extra-virgin olive oil.

3. Stir the pistou into the stew and let rest off the heat, covered, for a few minutes before serving. Serve immediately in warmed soup plates.

a really big chili

*Y*OU MAY think of chilis as stews of meat and beans, but in this instance pork is the star, in a flavorful sauce of vegetables and spicy chiles.

MAKES 8 SERVINGS

⅓ cup canola oil

3 lbs lean pork loin, cut into small dice

Salt as needed

Freshly ground black pepper as needed

2 cups small-dice yellow onions

2 tbsp minced garlic

4 cups chicken broth

¼ cup tomato purée

1 cup diced green chiles

2 fresh jalapeños, minced

3 tbsp mild pure chili powder, or to taste

3 tbsp ground cumin or to taste

2 tsp ground oregano

4 cups diced red-skinned potatoes, peeled

2 tbsp green Tabasco sauce

1 tsp white vinegar

1 cup grated Monterey Jack cheese

Four 8-inch flour tortillas, warmed

1. Heat the oil in a casserole or Dutch oven over high heat until it shimmers. Season the pork generously with salt and pepper. Add the pork to the hot oil, working in batches if necessary, and sauté, turning as necessary, until browned on all sides, 6 to 8 minutes. Transfer to a bowl and reserve.

2. Add the onions and garlic to the casserole and sauté, stirring frequently, until the onions are translucent, 6 to 8 minutes.

3. Add the broth, tomato purée, chiles, jalapeños, and the browned pork along with any juices it may have released to the casserole. Stir well and bring to a boil. Immediately reduce the heat to establish a gentle simmer.

4. Stir in half of chili powder, half of the cumin, and half of the oregano. Add the potatoes, green Tabasco, and vinegar and continue to simmer, adjusting the seasoning with additional chili powder, cumin, oregano, salt, and pepper, until the pork is fork tender, 1½ to 2 hours. Serve in heated bowls topped with the Monterey Jack and accompanied by the tortillas.

braises

bRAISES ARE ROBUST, hearty dishes that are incredibly accommodating when it comes to the ingredients you can use and the amount of time they cook. You can make most braises a day or two in advance; they actually taste better and have a better texture if they get to rest for a few days.

The Benefits of Braising

One of the primary benefits of the braising method is that less tender cuts of meat become tender as the moist heat gently penetrates the meat. The tough connective tissues soften and help to produce a full-bodied sauce. With the appropriate modifications and adaptations, even already-tender foods like seafood and vegetables can be braised successfully.

Most braised dishes take a relatively long time to cook properly, so you may want to save these dishes for times when you can be home for a longer period of time. But braises don't demand a lot of constant attention, just an occasional stir or skim as they sit on the stove or in the oven. All of the flavors, as well as the vitamins and minerals that escape from foods as they cook, are captured in the braising liquid, which is invariably served as a sauce with the dish. And you can get rid of most of the excess fat by carefully skimming braising dishes while they cook. To get rid of as much fat as possible, make the dish at least one day ahead and refrigerate it overnight. The fat will rise to the surface and harden enough to make it easy to spoon or lift it away from the braise before you reheat it.

Brown the Meat

The first step in many braises is to brown the surface of the meat or poultry in fat over high heat. This gives the food an appetizing color and also contributes good flavor to the final dish. Use a heavy-gauge ovenproof pan with a lid, such as a flameproof casserole or Dutch oven, that is just large enough to hold all the ingredients. Brown the meat in batches without crowding; you don't want to steam the meat in its own moisture. The meat should not be cooked through at this stage, and the browning should be done in the same pot that will be used for braising.

After the meat is browned, remove it from the pot and sauté a mixture of aromatics in the same fat (adding more oil or butter if needed). Mirepoix—a mixture of finely chopped onion, carrot, and celery—is commonly used to add a base of flavor. Other vegetables may be added, including mushrooms and tomatoes. Be sure to cook the vegetables until they release their flavorful liquid.

Add the Liquid and Return the Main Ingredient

Once all the aromatics are sautéed, add the braising liquid, typically a mixture of broth and wine. Whatever liquid you choose, remember that it should come only one-third of the way up the meat.

Cook Until Fork Tender and Finish the Sauce

Maintain a slow and gentle cooking speed in order to extract as much flavor as possible without drying out the food. When the meat is tender, remove it from the pot along with larger chunks of vegetables and keep it warm. Use a spoon or skimmer to degrease the liquid, skimming away as much of the floating fat as possible, in order to give the final sauce a better consistency. If the braising liquid is a little thin, bring it to a boil and let it reduce and thicken to a sauce-like consistency. If it is very thin, add just a drizzle of cornstarch slurry—a blend of cornstarch and water—and simmer until thickened.

braised lamb shanks

b RAISING IS often used for cooking leaner and tougher cuts of meat like lamb shanks, which braise beautifully. As the meat slowly cooks, the connective tissue dissolves, the meat becomes tender, and the juices develop into a rich sauce. Serve with couscous or rice pilaf to soak up every drop of the flavorful sauce.

MAKES 8 SERVINGS

4 tsp curry powder

1 tsp salt

1 tsp freshly ground black pepper, or as needed

1 tsp caraway seeds, crushed

1 tsp ground coriander

½ tsp ground cinnamon

½ tsp cayenne pepper

¼ tsp ground allspice

3 tbsp olive oil

8 lamb shanks (½ lb each)

2 cups thinly sliced yellow onion

1 cup diced green bell pepper

1 cup diced red bell pepper

2 tsp minced garlic

2 tbsp tomato paste

4 cups chicken broth

3 tbsp chopped raisins

6 dried apricots, slice thin

1. Preheat the oven to 325 degrees F.

2. Make a spice blend by stirring together the curry powder, salt, black pepper, caraway seeds, coriander, cinnamon, cayenne, and allspice in a small bowl. Rub 2 tablespoons of this spice blend evenly over the lamb shanks.

3. Heat the oil in a Dutch oven or flameproof casserole over medium-high heat. Place the lamb shanks in the casserole and sear, turning as necessary, until browned on all sides, about 10 minutes. Remove the lamb from casserole and set aside.

4. Add the onion, bell peppers, and garlic to the casserole. Sprinkle the vegetables with the remaining spice blend and stir until evenly coated. Sauté the vegetables until they are softened, about 10 minutes. Add the tomato paste and stir to combine. Add the broth, raisins, and apricots.

5. Return the lamb shanks to the casserole along with any juices they may have released and spoon some of the vegetables over the shanks. Cover the casserole and braise in the oven, turning the shanks occasionally to keep them moistened, until the lamb is cooked through and falling off the bone, about 2 hours. Remove the cover during the final 30 or 40 minutes of braising time to allow the sauce to reduce slightly. Skim away any fat from the surface and season to taste with salt and pepper. Serve the lamb shanks on heated plates covered with the sauce.

CLOCKWISE FROM UPPER LEFT When preparing to braise meats, they must first be seared; if vegetables are also being prepared, as is pictured here, the meat is removed from the pan to allow them room to cook properly, then added back later. When braising, the liquid in the pan shouldn't completely submerge the items being cooked. When finished cooking, braised meats are tender, moist, and should pull away easily from the bone. The finished Braised Lamb Shanks, pictured here with mashed potatoes, zucchini and carrots.

osso buco milanese

i N MILAN, osso buco is traditionally served on a bed of creamy saffron risotto (see note below) and topped with a pungent, colorful topping of garlic, lemon zest, parsley, and anchovies known as *gremolata*.

4 veal shank pieces, about 12 oz each

Salt as needed

Freshly ground black pepper as needed

Flour as needed for dredging veal shanks

3 tbsp olive oil

1 cup diced yellow onion

½ cup diced carrot

4 tsp minced garlic

3 tbsp tomato paste

¾ cup dry white wine

4 cups beef or chicken broth

1 tsp finely grated lemon zest

3 tbsp chopped flat-leaf parsley

2 anchovy fillets, chopped

1. Preheat the oven to 350 degrees F.

2. Season the veal shanks generously with salt and pepper. Dredge the shanks in flour and shake away any excess.

3. Heat the oil in an ovenproof casserole or Dutch oven over high heat until it shimmers. Sear the veal shanks in the oil, turning as necessary, until they have a good color on all sides, 10 to 12 minutes. Remove them to a platter and cover loosely with foil.

4. Add the onion, carrot, and 2 tsp minced garlic to the hot oil and sauté over medium heat, stirring frequently, until the onion is a deep golden brown, about 10 minutes. Add the tomato paste and sauté, stirring frequently, until the tomato paste turns a rust color, 2 to 3 minutes. Add the wine and stir well to dissolve the tomato paste.

5. Return the veal shanks to the casserole along with any juices they may have released and add enough broth to cover the shanks by about ½. Bring the broth to a simmer, cover the casserole, and place it in the oven. Braise the shanks, turning them as necessary to keep them evenly moistened, until they are very tender, about 1½ hours. Transfer the shanks to a serving platter and keep warm while finishing the sauce.

6. Strain the sauce, return it to the casserole, and bring it to a boil over high heat, skimming the surface as necessary. Reduce the heat to low simmer until the sauce has a lightly thickened consistency, about 10 minutes. Season to taste with salt and pepper.

7. Combine the remaining garlic, the lemon zest, parsley, and anchovy fillets to form the gremolata. Serve the shanks on heated plates garnished with the gremolata.

RISOTTO

A creamy risotto might make a main course, but for this Italian dish of braised veal, you might want to bend the rules of one dish cooking to be able to serve a traditional Italian-style side dish. Making risotto is not demanding—you can make it with ease while the veal shanks are braising.

For enough risotto to serve four, heat about 2 tablespoons of butter in a sauce pan. Add 1 cup of a round-grain rice such as Arborio or Carnaroli and stir the rice over medium heat. Add the broth, one cup at a time, until the rice has absorbed 3 cups of liquid. You should stir the risotto frequently

carbonnades of beef flamande

tHIS COMBINATION of beef and onions, cooked in dark, rich ale, is a classic example from the Belgians of how to make the most from the ingredients at hand. If you can find stout or porter, use it in this hearty braised dish. Broad noodles, steamed potatoes, or potato croquettes would make an excellent accompaniment to this dish.

MAKES 4 SERVINGS

4 beef chuck steaks (about 5 to 6 oz each)

Salt as needed

Freshly ground black pepper as needed

3 tbsp canola oil

4 medium-size yellow onions, sliced thick

2 tbsp tomato paste

¼ cup water

2 tbsp firmly packed dark brown sugar

12 oz dark beer

2 cups beef broth

1 tbsp Dijon-style mustard

2 tsp balsamic vinegar

1. Preheat oven to 300 degrees F.

2. Season the steaks generously with salt and pepper. Heat the oil in a cast-iron skillet over high heat until it shimmers.

Add the steaks to the skillet and sear them on both sides, about 2 minutes per side. Remove the steaks and hold them on a warmed plate.

3. Add the onions to the hot oil in the skillet and sauté them until they are a deep golden brown, 8 to 10 minutes. As they cook, stir them from time to time to prevent scorching.

4. Add the tomato paste to the onions and sauté for about 3 minutes over medium heat, stirring frequently. Add the water and brown sugar and stir well.

5. Add the beer and stir to blend. Allow the beer to reduce to half its original volume. Add the broth and bring the mixture to a simmer.

6. Return the steaks to the skillet along with any juices they have released. Cover the skillet and place in the oven. Braise the steaks, turning from time to time to keep them evenly moistened, until they are very tender, about 1½ hours.

7. Remove the steaks and keep them warm. Place the pan over medium heat and bring the sauce to a simmer. Remove any fat from the surface and add the mustard and balsamic vinegar. Allow the sauce to reduce slightly over high heat and adjust the seasoning with additional salt and pepper if necessary. Ladle the sauce over the steaks and serve on heated plates.

as it cooks to get a good creamy texture. (If you like, replace ½ cup of the broth with ½ cup dry white wine.) For a saffron risotto, add a few threads of crushed saffron with the first cup of broth.

Once the rice is tender and creamy, pull it off the heat and add 2 tablespoon butter and ⅓ to ½ cup grated Parmesan cheese. Stir the risotto vigorously until the butter and cheese are blended in. Serve at once on heated plates.

rabbit braised with fennel and garlic

Coniglio in Porchetta

THIS DISH calls for an unusual ingredient: wild fennel pollen. Fennel pollen gives the dish a unique flavor. Fennel grows wild throughout parts of the Mediterranean including Sicily, the region that gives us this dish. If you can't locate fennel pollen, use ground fennel seeds instead.

MAKES 8 SERVINGS

4 rabbits (2½ to 3 pounds each), with their livers

½ cup extra-virgin olive oil

½ tsp salt

1 tsp freshly ground black pepper, or as needed

4 sweet Italian sausages, casings removed

2 tsp minced garlic

½ cup dry white wine

4 tsp wild fennel pollen or ground fennel seed

4 medium-size fennel bulbs, cored and cut into wedges

1. Preheat the oven to 300 degrees F. Remove and coarsely chop the livers from the rabbits; reserve until needed. Cut the rabbits into pieces through the joints.

2. Heat 2 tablespoons of the oil in flameproof casserole or Dutch oven over high heat. Dry the rabbit pieces thoroughly, season with salt and pepper, and brown on all sides in the oil, turning as necessary, about 10 minutes. Transfer the rabbit from the casserole to a plate or pan and reserve.

3. Add the remaining oil to the casserole. Add the reserved rabbit livers, the sausage meat, and the garlic and sauté, stirring frequently to break up the sausage, until the sausage and livers have lost their raw appearance, about 10 minutes. Stir in the wine and fennel pollen or seed. Simmer over low heat until the wine reduces by about half. Season to taste with additional salt, pepper, or fennel.

4. Return the browned rabbit pieces along with any juices they may have released and the fennel to the casserole. Cover and place in the preheated oven and braise, turning the rabbit occasionally, until the rabbit and fennel are fork-tender, about 40 minutes.

braised rabbit with garganelli

Garganelli con Coniglio in Guazetto

Garganelli pasta, as a fresh pasta, is native to the Italian region of Romagna. Some versions of this pasta include grated cheese and nutmeg. The traditional way to serve garganelli is in a rich ragù, such as this braised rabbit dish. Its unusual name comes from a Latin word for trachea, *gargala*. Its shape is similar to a device used to examine the throat. Penne is a good substitute if you can't find garganelli.

MAKES 4 SERVINGS

½ oz dried porcini mushrooms

3 cups chicken broth or water, heated

2 tbsp olive oil

2 rabbits, quartered

Salt as needed

Freshly ground black pepper as needed

1 cup small-dice onion

½ cup small-dice carrot

½ cup small-dice celery

1 cup chopped plum tomato

1 tbsp tomato paste

1 cup dry white wine

2 bay leaves

1 sprig rosemary

2 cloves

½ lb garganelli or penne pasta, cooked al dente and drained

2 tbsp minced flat leaf parsley

Grated Parmesan as needed

1. Preheat the oven to 350 degrees F. Rehydrate the porcini in hot broth or water for 30 minutes. Strain the soaking liquid and set aside. Chop the mushrooms and set aside.

2. Heat the oil in flameproof casserole or Dutch oven over high heat. Dry the rabbit pieces thoroughly, season with salt and pepper, and brown on all sides in the oil, turning as necessary, about 10 minutes. Transfer the rabbit from the casserole to a plate or pan and reserve.

3. Add the onion, carrot, and celery to the casserole and sauté, stirring occasionally, until translucent, about 6 minutes. Add the chopped tomato and tomato paste and sauté, stirring constantly, until the tomato paste darkens in color and smells very sweet, about 2 minutes. Stir in the wine and simmer over low heat until the wine reduces by about half. Season to taste with additional salt and pepper.

4. Return the browned rabbit pieces, along with any juices they may have released, and the chopped porcinis to the casserole. Add the strained mushroom soaking liquid and enough additional broth or water to cover the rabbit pieces by one-third. Bring the braise to a simmer, add the bay leaves, rosemary sprig, and cloves, then immediately cover the casserole and place in the oven. Braise the rabbit, turning it occasionally, until it is fork-tender, about 45 minutes. Transfer the rabbit to a plate or dish and let it cool until it can be handled. Shred the rabbit meat and reserve.

5. Return the casserole to the medium-high heat, bring the sauce to a rapid simmer, and reduce, uncovered, until the sauce is thickened and flavorful, about 5 minutes. Remove and discard the bay leaves, rosemary sprig, and cloves. Return the shredded rabbit to the sauce and simmer until heated, about 5 minutes. Season to taste with additional salt and pepper. Spoon the rabbit and sauce over the garganelli or penne and serve very hot garnished with parsley and grated Parmesan cheese.

lamb with artichokes and spinach

in Avgolemono Sauce

*i*F YOU don't want to trim and cook the artichoke hearts yourself, look for frozen artichoke hearts. They will have a better flavor and add less salt to the dish than canned artichokes that have been packed in brine. If canned artichokes are all you can find, simply remember to rinse them with cold water before adding them to the dish.

MAKES 4 SERVINGS

¼ cup butter

1 tbsp extra-virgin olive oil

1½ lb boneless lamb shoulder, cut into large pieces

Salt as needed

Freshly ground black pepper as needed

1 cup chopped yellow onion

½ cup dry white wine

1 cup baby carrots

1½ cups water, or as needed

8 artichoke hearts, quartered

2 tbsp lemon juice

One 10-oz bag spinach, trimmed, cleaned, and chopped

2 tbsp chopped dill

2 large eggs

1. Heat the butter and olive oil in a large casserole over medium-high heat until the butter stops foaming. Season the lamb with salt and pepper and sear in the hot butter mixture, turning as necessary, until browned on all sides, about 10 minutes. Add the onion and sauté, stirring frequently, until the onion is tender and translucent, 6 to 8 minutes.

2. Add the wine, stir well to dissolve any drippings, and simmer until the wine has cooked away, about 5 minutes. Add the carrots and enough water to barely cover the lamb and carrots. Return to a simmer and then immediately reduce the heat to low until the dish is simmering gently. Cover the casserole and simmer, stirring occasionally and seasoning with additional salt and pepper, until the carrots are nearly tender, about 45 minutes.

3. Add the artichoke hearts and 1 teaspoon lemon juice to the casserole. Continue to simmer until the carrots and artichokes are tender, about 20 minutes. Add the spinach and dill, stir, and cook until the spinach is fully cooked, about 10 minutes.

4. Beat the eggs in a mixing bowl with a whisk until they are frothy. Pour in the remaining lemon juice while whisking the eggs. Slowly add about ½ cup of the hot sauce from the casserole to the eggs while whisking constantly and immediately pour the lemon sauce over the lamb. Swirl or shake the casserole over medium heat until thickened, about 12 minutes. Serve at once in heated bowls or plates.

braised beef short ribs

Kalbi Jim

KALBI JIM is a Korean dish made with short ribs that are cooked in a mirin-and-soy sauce until the sauce reduces to a mahogany glaze, and the meat is tender enough to fall from the bone.

MAKES 8 SERVINGS

8 beef short ribs, bone-in, cut into 3-inch lengths

Salt as needed

Freshly ground black pepper as needed

1½ cups mirin

¾ cup light soy sauce

2 cups large-dice yellow onion

2 slices ginger root (¼-inch-thick), peeled and lightly crushed

2 tsp minced garlic

½ cup jujube (Chinese red dates)

8 dried shiitake mushrooms, rehydrated and chopped, liquid reserved (see note)

2 cups sliced daikon

2 cups thinly sliced carrots, cut on diagonal

2 tsp sugar or as needed

¼ cup pine nuts, toasted

1 tbsp dark sesame oil

One 3-egg omelet, cut into diamonds or strips (see note)

1. Season the short ribs with salt and pepper and place in a casserole or Dutch oven. Add the mirin, soy sauce, onion, ginger, garlic, jujube, and reserved mushroom-infused water; there should be enough liquid to just cover ribs. Bring the liquid to a boil and then immediately lower the heat until the liquid is at a gentle simmer. Simmer, skimming as necessary and turning the ribs to keep them moist, until fork tender, about 2 hours.

2. When meat is fork tender add the mushrooms, daikon, and carrots and simmer until the vegetables are tender, about 10 minutes. Remove and discard the crushed ginger. Season to taste with additional soy sauce and sugar.

3. Stir in the pine nuts and sesame oil; simmer until heated through, about 5 minutes. Serve the ribs and vegetables on heated plates garnished with omelet diamonds or strips

REHYDRATING MUSHROOMS

Rehydrate dried mushrooms as follows: Place the mushrooms in a small bowl and add enough in warm water to cover them. Let them rest until they are softened, about 30 minutes. Lift the mushrooms from the water, letting it drain away. Save the liquid; you can strain it through a coffee filter and add it to any simmered dishes that could benefit from a touch of mushroom essence. You may need to cut away tough stems (especially with shiitake mushrooms). You can simply discard the stems, but if you make stocks and broths, you may want to save the stems to use in those recipes.

AN OMELET GARNISH

Several Asian recipes call for eggs. They may be stirred into soups or stir fries, but another popular option is making an omelet that can be cut into shapes.

First, heat a sauté pan over medium-high heat. Add enough oil to lubricate the pan well so the omelet won't stick. For this recipe, beat three eggs until they are frothy; the Chinese use chopsticks to avoid working in too much air. Season the eggs with a pinch of salt and pepper and pour them into the pan. The eggs will begin to set almost immediately. Use a heatproof spatula to push the cooked eggs away from the bottom. The uncooked eggs will flow to the bottom of the pan and cook. When the eggs are fully cooked, turn the omelet out of the pan onto a plate. Roll or fold it into a neat shape and let it rest until it is cool. Then, cut it into ribbons, diamonds, or other shapes.

marinated quail

Codornices "Marqués de Villena"

ALTHOUGH MOST braised dishes are served hot, this is a dish perfect to make and serve in the summer when the weather is sultry. Serve garnished with lemon wedges, pickles, and marinated hot peppers.

MAKES 4 SERVINGS

¼ cup olive oil

8 quail, trussed

20 pearl onions, peeled

1 garlic head, separated and peeled

3 carrots, cut in half crosswise and in quarters lengthwise

1 leek, cleaned

3 bay leaves

10 sprigs parsley

2 sprigs rosemary

4 sprigs thyme

Salt as needed

12 black peppercorns

1 celery stalk from the heart, with leaves still attached

⅛ teaspoon lightly crushed saffron threads

½ white wine vinegar

2 cups dry white wine

½ cup chicken broth

1 lemon, sliced thin

4 cornichons, cut into fans

1. Heat the oil in a large shallow casserole and sauté the quail slowly until they are brown on all sides. Transfer the birds to a warm platter.

2. In the same casserole, sauté the onions, garlic, carrots, and leek until the onions are wilted. Add the bay leaves, 2 sprigs parsley, rosemary, thyme, salt, peppercorns, celery, and saffron. Stir in the vinegar, wine, and chicken broth. Return the quail to the casserole. Cover and simmer for 45 minutes. Cool, cover, and refrigerate, turning the quail occasionally, until well-chilled, at least 2 and up to 12 hours.

3. To serve, bring the quail to room temperature and cut in halves. Remove and discard the leek, parsley, peppercorns, and celery. Julienne the cooked carrots and reserve. Return the quail skin side up to the marinade and arrange attractively with the carrots, pearl onions, the remaining parsley sprigs, sliced lemon, and cornichons.

chicken with okra

CHICKEN PIECES braise in an aromatic tomato sauce with okra in this intensely flavored dish. Giving the okra a quick flash in the hot oil adds an interesting texture and flavor that you might not expect.

MAKES 4 SERVINGS

Salt as needed

¾ lb small okra pods, trimmed (see note below)

3 tbsp cider vinegar

¼ cup olive oil

4 whole chicken legs (drumsticks and thighs)

¾ cup minced onion

¼ cup minced green frying pepper

½ tsp dried oregano

⅛ tsp hot pepper flakes

1 pinch cinnamon

2 cups diced plum tomatoes

¾ tsp sugar, or as needed

2 tbsp lemon juice, or as needed

Freshly ground black pepper as needed

½ cup chicken broth or water or as needed

3 tbsp chopped parsley

1. Fill a small dish with enough salt to make an even layer, about ¼ inch deep. Dip the trimmed ends of the okra into salt. Put the okra in a single layer on a baking sheet and sprinkle with the vinegar. Let the okra rest at room temperature for 1 hour. Rinse the okra and let it dry.

2. Preheat the oven to 375 degrees F.

3. Heat half of the oil in a casserole or Dutch oven over medium-high heat until it shimmers. Sear the chicken in the oil, turning as necessary, until the chicken is lightly colored on all sides, 8 to 10 minutes. Transfer to a plate and keep warm.

4. Add as much of the remaining oil as needed to generously coat the casserole. Add the okra (working in batches to avoid crowding the pan) and sear on all sides until brown, about 4 minutes. Transfer to a plate and keep warm.

5. Add the onion and pepper to the casserole and sauté over medium heat, stirring frequently, until the onion is golden brown, about 10 minutes. Add the oregano, pepper flakes and cinnamon; sauté, stirring frequently, until aromatic, about 30 seconds. Add the tomatoes and cook until soft, thick, and lightly caramelized, about 10 minutes. Season to taste with the sugar, lemon juice, and additional salt and pepper.

6. Add the okra to the tomato sauce, pushing them under the surface, then arrange the chicken pieces on top of the okra. Add enough broth or water to bring the level of the liquid up to partially cover the chicken pieces. Bring the sauce up to a simmer. Immediately cover the casserole, transfer to the oven, and braise, basting the chicken legs occasionally, until the chicken is tender, about 45 minutes.

7. Transfer the chicken to a heated platter or plates. Return the casserole to high heat and simmer long enough to slightly reduce the sauce. Skim away any fat that rises to the surface and season to taste with additional lemon juice, salt, and pepper.

8. Ladle the sauce over the chicken pieces, sprinkle with parsley, and serve at once.

OKRA

Choose small, young okra pods that are no more than 3 inches long. The pods should be clean and fresh; the pods will snap crisply when you bend them in half. Over-the-hill okra looks dull and dry.

Keep okra dry until just before you cook it; moisture will cause the pods to become slimy. You can store untrimmed, uncut okra in a paper or plastic bag in the refrigerator crisper drawer for up to three days, so plan on preparing okra very soon after you buy it.

chicken smothered in green olives

Cooks in North Africa rub the entire bird, inside and out, with a paste of garlic and salt, to both flavor and purify the bird before they prepare it. You can just as easily make this dish with chicken pieces instead of a whole bird.

MAKES 4 SERVINGS

3 garlic cloves, peeled

Salt as needed

1 roasting chicken, about 3½ lb

3 tbsp peanut or olive oil

½ cup minced yellow onion

1½ tsp minced garlic

½ tsp freshly ground black pepper, or as needed

½ tsp ground ginger

¼ tsp turmeric

¼ tsp ground cumin

¼ tsp sweet paprika

2 cups chicken broth or water

½ cup green olives, drained and pitted

1 tbsp lemon juice, or more to taste

3 tbsp chopped flat-leaf parsley

2 tbsp chopped cilantro

1. Preheat the oven to 325 degrees F.

2. Crush the 3 cloves of garlic with the side of your knife. Sprinkle about 2 teaspoons of salt over the garlic and chop very fine. Use the side of your blade to scrape the garlic and salt together until a paste forms. Rub the paste evenly over the inside and outside of the chicken. Put the chicken in a pan and let it rest in the refrigerator for 30 minutes. Rinse the garlic paste from the chicken thoroughly and pat dry.

3. Heat the oil in a tagine or casserole over medium-high heat until it shimmers. Sear the chicken in the oil, turning as necessary, until the chicken is lightly colored on all sides, 8 to 10 minutes. Transfer to a plate and keep warm.

4. Add the onion to the tagine or casserole and sauté over medium heat, stirring frequently, until the onion is translucent, about 6 minutes. Add the garlic and sauté, stirring occasionally, until aromatic, about 1 minute. Add ½ teaspoon ground black pepper, the ginger, turmeric, cumin, and paprika to the tagine and sauté, stirring constantly, until aromatic, about 30 seconds.

5. Return the chicken to the tagine along with any juices it may have released and add enough broth or water to cover the chicken by about one-third. Bring the broth to a boil. Cover the tagine and transfer to the oven. Braise, turning the chicken occasionally, until halfway done, about 30 minutes. Add the olives and lemon juice, stirring them into the sauce, and continue to simmer until the chicken is very tender and the sauce is flavorful, about 30 minutes. Add a little more broth as needed throughout the cooking time to keep the chicken evenly moistened.

6. Remove the chicken to a heated plate and keep warm. Place the tagine or casserole over medium heat and bring the sauce to a simmer. Remove any fat from the surface and add the parsley and cilantro. Allow the sauce to reduce slightly over high heat. Season to taste with salt and pepper. Divide the chicken into serving pieces and serve on heated plates with the olive sauce.

When you are ready to prepare the okra, rinse it in plenty of cool running water and let it drain in a colander. If the pods are very fuzzy, rub them in a kitchen towel or with a vegetable brush to remove some of the fuzz.

To cook okra whole, as for Chicken with Okra, trim a very thin slice from both the stem end and tip but don't pierce the internal capsule; prepared this way, the juices won't be released and the okra won't become gummy. When you are cutting okra into slices, however, you can trim the stem end more deeply.

chicken mole

Mole Poblano de Pollo

*i*N OAXACA, a state in southeastern Mexico, you can find dozens of different kinds of moles. Some even claim that mole got its start in Oaxaca. While chocolate may be the best-known ingredient in some mole sauces, it's really just a grace note in this rich harmony of spices, chiles, nuts, and seeds.

MAKES 4 SERVINGS

3 tbsp olive oil

4 chicken legs (thigh and drumstick)

Salt as needed

Freshly ground pepper as needed

1 yellow onion, finely diced

1 green bell pepper, finely diced

1 jalapeño, finely chopped

¼ cup blanched almonds, chopped

3 garlic cloves, smashed

2 tbsp chili powder

1 tsp grated ginger root

½ tsp minced thyme

¼ tsp aniseed

¼ tsp ground cinnamon

3 plum tomatoes, peeled, seeded, and chopped

1 cup chicken broth, plus more as needed

3 tbsp almond butter

2 tablets Mexican chocolate, chopped (see note)

2 tbsp toasted sesame seeds

1. Preheat the oven to 350 degrees F.
2. Heat the oil in a large Dutch oven over medium-high heat. Season the chicken with salt and pepper and then sear, turning as necessary, until browned on all sides, about 10 minutes. Remove and set aside.
3. Add the onion to the hot pan and sauté, stirring frequently, until golden brown, 10 to 12 minutes. Add the bell pepper, jalapeño, almonds, and garlic to the pan and sauté until aromatic, 3 to 4 minutes. Add the chili powder, ginger, thyme, aniseed, and cinnamon and sauté until aromatic, about 30 seconds, being careful not to burn the mixture. Add the tomatoes and stir to combine.
4. Pour in 1 cup of the broth and stir to dissolve any browned bits in the pan. Whisk in the almond butter, return the chicken to the pan along with any juices it may have released, and bring to a boil. Cover the pan and transfer to the oven. Braise the chicken, turning it occasionally, until tender, about 1 hour. Add a little more broth as needed throughout the cooking time to keep the chicken evenly moistened.
5. Remove the chicken from the pot and cover to keep warm. Add the chocolate to the sauce, stirring until melted. Season to taste with additional salt and pepper.
6. Return the chicken to the sauce and turn to coat evenly. Bring the mixture to a simmer over medium heat to heat the chicken through, and then serve at once. Garnish with the sesame seeds.

MEXICAN CHOCOLATE

Look for flat cakes of Mexican chocolate, flavored with sugar, cinnamon, and finely ground almonds, in the ethnic foods section of large supermarkets or in groceries specializing in Latin American foods.

seafood and meat paella

Paella de Mariscos y Carne

i N SPAIN, a paella is an outdoor event. Large paella pans, some more than three feet in diameter, are set over open wood fires. The dish takes on a wonderful smoky flavor from the fire. Calasparra rice is the most authentic choice for this dish; it has been used since it arrived with the Moors in the Middle Ages. If you can't find it, however, use the same kind of rice you'd choose for a risotto. For information on how to prepare the mussels and clams for cooking, see the note "Cooking with Mussels and Clams" on page 119.

MAKES 6 SERVINGS

¼ cup olive oil

3 whole chicken breasts, halved

3 whole chicken legs, cut into drumsticks and thighs

2 lb boneless pork roast, cut into 2-inch cubes

Salt as needed

Freshly ground black pepper as needed

½ lb squid, bodies sliced in rings, tentacles coarsely chopped

1 cup chopped green bell pepper

1 cup chopped plum tomato

2 tsp minced garlic

2½ cups round-grain rice

½ tsp saffron threads, lightly crushed

5 cups chicken broth

½ cup dry white wine

½ cup fresh or frozen peas

5 piquillo peppers, cut into julienne

2 dozen mussels

2 dozen littleneck clams

12 jumbo shrimp, in the shell (see note)

2 tsp lemon juice

1. Preheat the oven to 350 degrees F.

2. Heat the oil in a paella pan or deep skillet over medium-high heat until it shimmers. Season the chicken and pork with salt and pepper; working in batches, sear in the hot oil, turning as necessary, until browned on all sides, about 12 minutes.

3. Add the squid, green pepper, tomato, and garlic. Cook, stirring frequently, until the squid becomes opaque, about 3 minutes. Add the rice and saffron, stir to coat evenly, and sauté until the rice begins to change color slightly, about 4 minutes. Add the broth and wine; bring to a boil over high heat, then reduce the heat to a slow simmer.

4. Add the peas and piquillo peppers, and arrange the mussels, clams, and shrimp on top of the paella. Sprinkle with lemon juice. Cover the pan or skillet and transfer to the oven. Cook until and the rice has absorbed the broth and the clams and mussels open, 15 to 20 minutes. Discard any shells that do not open. Let the paella rest for 5 minutes before serving directly from the paella pan or skillet.

ABOUT SHRIMP

If you can find jumbo shrimp with the heads on, show them off in this dish. You may need to teach the uninitiated how to twist away the tail, pull off the shell, and then suck out the juices from the head. Have plenty of napkins on hand if this is a family-and-friends affair. For a more elegant dining experience, however, put out finger bowls with a thin slice of lemon to rinse off your fingertips.

chicken with almonds and chick peas

Djeg Kdra

a TRADITIONAL MOROCCAN dish, *kdra* is a slowly braised dish made in a tagine. Tagines have cone-shaped lids that capture the steam released by the dish as it cooks. The steam falls back onto the food, basting and flavoring it throughout the cooking time.

MAKES 4 SERVINGS

1 cup whole almonds, blanched

3 or 4 saffron threads

¼ tsp ground turmeric

2 tbsp clarified butter or smen (see note, page 47)

4 chicken legs (drumstick and thigh)

Salt as needed

Freshly ground black pepper as needed

½ tsp ground ginger

1 cinnamon stick

½ cup minced yellow onion

2 cups thinly sliced yellow onion

½ cup cooked chick peas, drained and rinsed

4 cups chicken broth or as needed

¼ cup chopped flat-leaf parsley

2 tsp lemon juice or as needed

1. Place the almonds in a small sauce pan and add enough cold water to cover them. Bring to a gentle simmer over low heat, cover, and immediately remove from the heat. Let the almonds soak in the hot water until softened, about 1 hour.

2. Crush the saffron threads together with the ground turmeric in a small dish and reserve.

3. Heat the butter or smen in a casserole or tagine over medium-high heat until hot but not smoking. Season the chicken with salt and pepper and sear in the hot butter, turning as necessary, until the chicken is lightly colored on all sides, 8 to 10 minutes. Transfer to a plate and keep warm.

4. Add half of the saffron-turmeric mixture, the ginger, and cinnamon stick to the butter in the casserole and sauté, stirring constantly, until aromatic, about 30 seconds. Add the minced onion and sauté, stirring frequently, until the onion is translucent, about 6 minutes.

5. Add the reserved chicken along with any juices it may have released, the sliced onion, and chick peas to the casserole or tagine. Add enough of the broth to barely cover the chicken. Cover the casserole and braise over very low heat until the chicken is very tender, 45 to 50 minutes.

6. Drain the almonds and add them to the sauce, along with the parsley and the remaining saffron-turmeric mixture. Simmer the sauce long enough to heat the almonds, 1 to 2 minutes. Season to taste with lemon juice and additional salt and pepper. Serve directly from the tagine or casserole on heated plates.

SMEN

Smen is a traditional butter-based cooking oil featured in Moroccan dishes. It is made in the same basic manner as ghee (page xxx), but instead of using butter made from cow milk, smen is made from sheep or goat milk. While you may think of butter as something perishable, this preserved butter is prepared in such a way that it can last for several months. The deep, pungent aroma is used to enhance many savory dishes, especially couscous.

braised monkfish with cumin-scented beans

Peskandritsa me Ospria Kai Kimino

MONKFISH HOLDS up beautifully when you braise it. You could substitute a variety of other beans or even lentils for those we've included here.

MAKES 4 SERVINGS

2 tbsp olive oil

2½ lb monkfish fillet

Salt as needed

Freshly ground black pepper as needed

2 cups chopped yellow onion

2 celery stalks, medium dice

1 fennel bulb, medium dice

½ tsp minced garlic

½ cup cooked navy beans, drained and rinsed

½ cup cooked chick peas, drained and rinsed

½ cup cooked fava beans, drained and rinsed

½ cup wheat kernels, soaked

2 to 3 cups fish broth

1 tbsp cumin

3 to 4 tbsp vinegar

2 tbsp minced thyme

1. Preheat the oven to 325 degrees F.

2. Heat the oil in a casserole or Dutch oven over high heat until it shimmers. Season the monkfish with salt and pepper and cook in the hot oil until the fish is lightly colored on all sides, about 10 minutes. Transfer to a dish and keep warm.

3. Add the onion, celery, fennel, and garlic and sauté, stirring occasionally, until the onion is translucent, about 6 minutes. Add the beans and wheat and enough fish broth to cover them by about ½ inch. Bring to a simmer over high heat and cook until the wheat is nearly tender, about 20 minutes. Season to taste with cumin, vinegar, salt, and pepper.

4. Return the monkfish to the casserole, setting it on top of the beans and wheat. Sprinkle the thyme over the fish, cover, and braise in the oven until the fish is cooked through and the wheat is very tender, 15 to 20 minutes. Slice the fish and serve on a bed of the beans.

crawfish étouffée

é TOUFFÉE IS the name given to dishes like this one that are gently cooked in a covered pot. Crawfish, or crayfish, are sold live or as cooked meat. If you buy crawfish meat, look for the words fat-on. Crawfish fat is an integral part of a good étouffée.

MAKES 5 SERVINGS

3 tbsp bacon fat or canola oil

1½ cups minced onion

1 cup minced celery

¾ cup minced green bell pepper

2 tsp minced garlic

1 tbsp mild paprika

¼ tsp ground white pepper

¼ tsp freshly ground black pepper, or as needed

⅛ tsp ground cayenne

Salt as needed

¼ cup all-purpose flour

2 cups fish or chicken broth or as needed

1¼ lb crawfish tail meat with fat

3 tbsp butter

1 cup thinly sliced scallions, white and green portions

¼ cup basil chiffonade

2 tbsp chopped flat-leaf parsley

1. Heat the bacon fat or oil in a casserole or Dutch oven over medium heat until it shimmers.

2. Add the onion to the tagine or casserole and sauté over medium heat, stirring frequently, until the onion is translucent, about 6 minutes. Add the celery, bell pepper, and garlic; cover the pan and cook over low heat, stirring occasionally, until the vegetables are tender and translucent, about 10 minutes. Add the paprika, white and black pepper, cayenne, and ½ teaspoon salt; sauté, stirring constantly, until aromatic, about 1 minute.

3. Sprinkle the flour over the vegetables and continue to cook, stirring constantly, until the mixture is thick and pasty, about 3 minutes. Add the broth and stir well to work out any lumps. Bring to a simmer over medium heat. Add the crawfish tails and their fat. Cover the pot and cook over very low heat, stirring frequently, until the crawfish is cooked through and very hot, 8 to 10 minutes. Add a little more broth as needed throughout the cooking time if the étouffé is getting too thick. Season to taste with additional salt and pepper.

4. Add the butter, scallions, basil, and parsley and stir to combine. Serve the étouffée in heated bowls.

feijoada

Meat Stew with Black Beans

bRAZILIANS TYPICALLY enjoy this hearty meal at midday, accompanied by a *caipirinha* and followed by a nap. Plan on spending two or three days putting this magnificent dish together. Serve feijoada with steamed rice, braised greens, and sliced oranges for a traditional presentation.

MAKES 8 TO 10 SERVINGS

1½ cups dry black beans, rinsed and sorted

1 lb carne seca (page 23) or corned beef

2 lb smoked pork spareribs or smoked pork chops

¾ lb slab bacon

1½ lb boneless beef chuck or eye round

1 ham hock

1 pig's foot, split

10 to 12 cups low sodium or homemade chicken broth or water

1 bay leaf

Salt as needed

2 tbsp peanut or olive oil

1½ cups minced onion

¼ lb chorizo, sliced ¼ inch thick

2 tsp minced garlic

½ cup thinly sliced scallions, cut on the diagonal

1 jalapeño, seeded and minced

Freshly ground black pepper as needed

1. Soak the black beans in enough cold water to cover generously for at least 6 and up to 12 hours in the refrigerator. In a separate container, soak the corned beef in the refrigerator overnight in enough cold water to cover.

2. Drain the corned beef and place it in large Dutch oven along with the smoked spareribs or chops, bacon, beef, ham hock, and pig's foot. Add enough broth or water to cover the meats. Add the bay leaf, cover the Dutch oven, and bring the broth to a simmer over low heat, skimming as necessary. Simmer until the meats are all tender, removing them from the broth as they become fork-tender (1 hour for the spareribs and ham hocks; 1½ to 2 hours to 1 hour for the other meats), and transfer them to a bowl. When all of the meat has been removed from the Dutch oven, strain the broth. (You can cool the meats and broth now and continue the cooking the next day.)

3. Drain the soaked beans and rinse well. Place them in the Dutch oven and add enough of the strained broth to cover the beans. Bring the broth to a boil over medium-high heat and then immediately reduce the heat for a slow simmer, skimming as necessary, until the beans are tender and creamy to the bite, 1½ to 2 hours. Season to taste with salt. Drain the beans, reserving their cooking liquid separately.

4. Heat the oil the Dutch oven over medium heat until it shimmers. Sauté the onion in the oil, stirring frequently, until golden, about 10 minutes. Add the chorizo, garlic, scallions, and jalapeño; sauté, stirring frequently, until very hot and aromatic, about 5 minutes. Return the drained beans to the Dutch oven along with enough of the strained liquid from the beans to make a good, stew-like consistency. Simmer until the feijoada is very flavorful, 10 to 15 minutes. Lightly mash some of the beans with the back of a spoon to thicken the sauce, if desired. Season to taste with salt and pepper.

5. Remove the meat from the ham hocks and cut it into medium dice. Remove the rind from the bacon and cut it into a medium dice. Add the diced ham and bacon to the beans and simmer 15 minutes. Slice the corned beef, beef, and separate the spareribs into portions. Add them to the beans and continue to simmer until the feijoada is very flavorful and thickened, about 15 minutes. Serve on heated plates.

veal braised in asti spumante

asti spumante, or simply Asti, is an effervescent, fruity wine, from the Piedmont region of Italy, made from the Muscat grape. We've included both white and cremini mushrooms in this dish, but feel free to use whatever mushrooms look good at the market—exotic varieties add intriguing flavors and shapes to the dish.

MAKES 6 SERVINGS

3 lb boneless veal shoulder roast or veal breast, rolled and tied

Salt as needed

Freshly ground black pepper as needed

¼ cup olive oil

1 cup chopped onion

2 cups sliced white mushrooms

1 cup sliced cremini mushrooms

1½ cups Asti spumante

2 cups beef broth, as needed

1 cup seedless green grapes, halved

1. Preheat the oven to 350 degrees F.
2. Season the veal roast with salt and pepper. Heat the olive oil in a large Dutch oven over high heat until it shimmers. Sear the veal in the hot oil, turning occasionally, until golden brown on all sides, about 10 minutes. Transfer to a pan and keep warm.
3. Reduce the heat to medium, add the onion to the pan, and cook slowly until tender and golden brown, about 15 minutes. Add the sliced mushrooms and continue to sauté until the moisture they release cooks away, about 10 minutes.
4. Add the Asti spumante and stir well to dissolve the drippings. Simmer over high heat until the Asti spumante reduces by half. Return the veal to the Dutch oven and add enough broth to come about halfway up the sides of the veal.
5. Cover the Dutch oven and braise the veal in the oven, turning as necessary to keep the veal evenly moistened, until it is tender, about 2½ to 3 hours. Add the grapes to the sauce and continue to simmer until the grapes are hot and the veal is fork-tender, about 30 minutes.
6. Transfer the meat to a warm pan or plate, coat with some of the braising liquid, and set aside to stay warm. Return the Dutch oven to medium-high heat and simmer the sauce, skimming as necessary, until it thickens slightly, about 10 minutes. Season to taste with additional salt and pepper. Slice the veal and serve with the sauce.

pastas and baked dishes

THE RECIPES IN this chapter run the gamut from simple-to-assemble dishes for quick and easy dinners on a busy night to classic dishes that incorporate sauces, vegetables, stews, and toppings like pastry crusts. Many baked dishes and casseroles are traditionally baked in single large casseroles or baking pans, but you may choose to layer them into individual dishes for single servings to enjoy now or freeze for later.

Cooking Pasta

Pasta, whether it is fresh or dry, is simple to cook. In the best of all possible worlds, your pasta comes directly from the pot at the same moment that your sauce is ready. Hot, freshly cooked pasta can absorb the sauce more readily for a better-tasting pasta dish.

To cook pasta properly you need a large pot with plenty of boiling water, some salt, and a colander. The ratio of water to pasta is about 4 quarts of water for every 1 pound of pasta with 1 to 2 tablespoons of salt. Using a lot of water gives the pasta plenty of room to cook properly, so it won't stick together as much. The water will come back to a boil more quickly if there is lots of it and that is what you want. Adding a generous quantity of salt to the cooking water is important for the best flavor in the finished dish.

Once you add the pasta to the pot, stir it a few times at the start of cooking time to separate the pasta, especially long pastas like spaghetti or linguini. After that you can leave the pasta to cook on its own. Read the label on the box to learn the suggested cooking time, but be sure that you also test the pasta for doneness by biting or cutting into a piece. If you see a white core at the center of the pasta, it needs to cook a little longer.

Lift the pot carefully from the stove and pour the contents into a colander that you've already set up in your sink. Let the pasta drain and give the colander a few shakes to remove any water that remains. Shaped pasta like penne or orechiette can trap water, so be vigilant. Extra water on the pasta means less flavor from your sauce.

Restaurants often have to prepare large quantities of pasta ahead of time in order to manage their dinner service properly. You can use those techniques at home to make last-minute assembly of pasta dishes less hectic. Remember that there is a slight tradeoff: Adding oil to the pasta makes it more difficult for the sauce to cling.

Undercook the pasta slightly, then drain as directed above. Once the pasta is drained, run plenty of cold water over the pasta, turning it until it cools. Let the water drain away and then, with scrupulously clean hands, toss a tablespoon or so of olive oil into the pasta, but don't use too much. This will keep the pasta from sticking together in a big mass.

When you are ready to serve the pasta, bring about 2 inches of salted water to a rapid boil in a large sauce pot. Add the pasta to the boiling water, simmer until the pasta is very hot, about 2 to 3 minutes, then drain and sauce as normal.

vegetarian moussaka

Seitan is a protein-rich food made from wheat, with a dense, meaty texture that makes it an ideal vegetarian substitute in traditionally meat-based dishes. You can find it in the produce section of many larger supermarkets, or in natural or health food stores.

MAKES 8 SERVINGS

3 lb eggplant (2 large or 3 medium)

2 tsp kosher salt, to taste

3 tbsp butter

¼ cup flour

3 cups milk

½ tsp ground black pepper, to taste

1½ lb potatoes

3 tbsp olive oil, or as needed

1 cup minced onion

1½ teaspoons minced garlic

2 cups chopped plum tomatoes

1 cup dry white wine

6 cups vegetable broth

2 cups crumbled seitan

⅓ cup dark raisins

¼ cup toasted pine nuts

2 tbsp chopped flat-leaf parsley

2 tsp chopped thyme

2 tsp chopped oregano

1 tsp ground cinnamon

2 egg yolks, beaten

1. Peel and slice the eggplant about ¼ inch thick. Place in a colander, sprinkle liberally with kosher salt, and let rest until the salt begins to draw out some of the liquid, about 20 minutes. Rinse the eggplant thoroughly, let drain, and blot dry. (see note "Preparing Eggplant for Cooking" on page 113)

2. While the eggplant is draining, prepare a white sauce: Melt the butter in a saucepan over medium heat. Add the flour and stir well to make a smooth paste. Continue to cook, stirring frequently, until the mixture has a light blond color, 5 to 6 minutes. Add the milk gradually, whisking as you add it, until it is all incorporated and the sauce is smooth. Simmer over medium-low to low heat until the sauce is thick and smooth. Taste and adjust the seasoning with salt and pepper. Remove from the heat and reserve.

3. Put the potatoes in a pot and add enough water to cover them; bring to a simmer over medium-high heat. Simmer until a skewer or paring knife can be easily inserted about halfway into the potato, about 20 minutes. Drain the potatoes and set aside until they are cool enough to handle. Remove the skin and slice the potatoes into ¼-inch-thick rounds; set aside.

4. Heat 2 tablespoons oil in a skillet over medium high heat. Add the eggplant slices in batches (do not allow the slices to touch or pile up on top of each other). Fry on the first side until a light golden brown, about 2 minutes. Turn and fry on the second side until golden brown, another 2 minutes. As the slices are cooked, remove them to a paper lined pan to absorb any excess oil. Add more oil to the pan as necessary as you fry the eggplant. Continue to fry until all of the slices are done. Set aside. *(recipe continues on page 112)*

CLOCKWISE FROM UPPER LEFT *Keeping the eggplant slices in a single layer in the pan, sauté until golden brown. When assembling the moussaka, make sure that the eggplant and potato slices are evenly spaced and layered. Add the white sauce to the dish one ladle at a time, allowing it a chance to infuse through the layered vegetables and reach the bottom; if desired, you could also gently tap the bottom of the dish against a hard surface to force any trapped air out of the casserole. The finished moussaka should have a slightly bubbly sauce and rich golden brown color.*

5. In the same pan, heat enough of the oil to generously coat the pan until the oil shimmers. Add the onion and sauté, stirring frequently, until golden brown, about 10 to 12 minutes. Add the garlic and continue to sauté, stirring frequently, until there is a good aroma from the garlic, another 1 or 2 minutes. Add the tomatoes and cook over medium heat, stirring from time to time, until the tomatoes have a rich aroma and turn a deep rust color, 5 to 6 minutes. Add the wine and broth and simmer until the liquid reduces by about half. Add the crumbled seitan and continue to cook just until evenly moistened and heated through, about 2 minutes. Stir in the raisins, pine nuts, parsley, thyme, oregano, and cinnamon. Taste the mixture and adjust as necessary with salt and pepper.

6. Preheat the oven to 350°F.

7. To assemble the moussaka, brush a casserole or baking dish with oil. Add a thin layer of the seitan mixture, followed by a layer of potatoes, then another thin layer of the seitan mixture, followed by a layer of eggplant. Continue to layer in this sequence until you have used all of the ingredients, ending with a layer of the seitan.

8. Blend the egg yolks into the white sauce and pour in an even layer over the top of the moussaka. Bake until the potatoes are very tender and easy to pierce with the tip of a paring knife, 1 to 1¼ hours. (Cover the moussaka loosely with foil if the top layer is browning too quickly.)

9. Remove the moussaka from the oven and let it rest for 15 minutes before slicing and serving.

lamb and eggplant moussaka

mAKING MOUSSAKA is something of an undertaking—a rich meat sauce (made here with lamb, but you can substitute other ground meats such as turkey, veal, or even pork, if you prefer), layered with tender eggplant and a cheese sauce. You can make the moussaka in two smaller casserole dishes to serve one now and freeze one to bake later.

MAKES 12 TO 14 SERVINGS

3 lb eggplant (2 large or 3 medium)

Salt as needed

⅓ cup olive oil, or as needed

2 cups diced onion

1¼ lb ground lamb (or substitute beef, turkey, pork, or combination)

2 cups chopped plum tomatoes

2 tsp minced garlic

2 cloves

Small piece cinnamon stick (or ¼ tsp ground cinnamon)

1 bay leaf

Pinch ground allspice

Freshly ground black pepper, as needed

½ cup water

2 tbsp tomato paste

¼ cup dry red wine

¼ cup plain bread crumbs

2 cups Cheese Sauce (recipe follows)

1. Peel, salt, and rinse the eggplant if desired (see note "Preparing Eggplant for Cooking" below).

2. Heat about 1 tablespoon of olive oil in a skillet over medium-high heat until it shimmers. Add the eggplant to the hot oil a few slices at a time and sauté the eggplant slices, turning as necessary, until tender and lightly colored, 2 to 3 minutes on each side. Transfer to a rack to drain while you sauté the remaining eggplant, adding more oil to the skillet as necessary.

3. To prepare a meat sauce: Heat 1 tablespoon of olive oil in a skillet. Add the onion and cook over medium high heat, stirring frequently, until tender, 10 to 12 minutes. Add the ground meat and cook over medium heat, stirring frequently, until the meat loses its raw appearance, about 5 minutes. Add the tomatoes, garlic, cloves, cinnamon, bay leaf, allspice, salt, pepper, and about ½ cup water. Simmer until thick and flavorful, about 30 minutes. Add the tomato paste and red wine and continue simmering until the wine has developed a sweet aroma, about 10 minutes.

4. Preheat the oven to 350 degrees F.

5. To assemble the moussaka: Scatter the bread crumbs in a deep, rectangular baking dish. Place a layer of half of the eggplant slices over the bread crumbs. Add the meat sauce and spread it into an even layer. Add the remaining eggplant in an even layer over the meat sauce. Pour the cheese sauce over the eggplant. Bake, uncovered, until the cheese sauce is thick and golden brown and the eggplant is very tender, about 45 minutes. Let the moussaka rest for about 20 minutes before cutting and serving.

PREPARING EGGPLANT FOR COOKING

Many recipes instruct you to salt eggplant before you cook it. Some say this step is necessary because it draws out any bitterness in the eggplant. We think it's a good idea, even if the eggplant isn't large or bitter. Drawing out some of the moisture in eggplant collapses the vegetable a little, so it doesn't act as much like a sponge for oil when you fry it.

Cheese Sauce

MAKES 2 CUPS

5 tbsp butter

5 tbsp all-purpose flour

2½ cups milk

Few grains of nutmeg

Salt as needed

Freshly ground black pepper as needed

2 egg yolks

½ cup grated kefalotyri or Parmesan cheese

1. Heat the butter in a saucepan over medium heat. Add the flour and stir well. Cook for about 5 minutes, stirring constantly. Gradually whisk in the milk, working out any lumps that form. Bring to a full boil, then reduce the heat to low and gently simmer, stirring frequently, until thickened, about 30 minutes.

2. Remove the sauce from the heat and add nutmeg, salt, and pepper to taste. Whisk the egg yolks in a small boil and add a bit of the hot sauce to the yolks. Blend well, and return the yolk mixture to the rest of the béchamel. Stir in the cheese and blend well. Keep warm while preparing the moussaka.

Peel the eggplant if you wish and slice the eggplant to the required thickness. Place the slices in a colander and put the colander in a large bowl. Sprinkle the slices liberally with kosher salt and let them rest until the salt begins to draw moisture to the surface, about 20 minutes. Rinse the eggplant thoroughly, let drain, and blot dry.

vegetable lasagna

i N THIS vegetable lasagna, noodles are layered with sliced eggplant and zucchini and a ricotta "custard" made with ricotta and eggs. You can use reduced-fat versions of mozzarella and ricotta in this dish without sacrificing flavor.

MAKES 8 SERVINGS

1¼ lb sliced eggplant (about 1 large or 2 medium)

1¼ lb sliced zucchini (about 3 medium)

Salt as needed

Freshly ground black pepper as needed

⅓ cup olive oil, or as needed

2 cups sliced shiitake mushrooms

12 cups sliced white mushrooms

¼ tsp garlic powder, or to taste

1 cup grated Parmesan cheese

2 cups ricotta cheese

2 large eggs

1 tbsp chopped flat-leaf parsley

12 dry lasagna noodles

2 cups Tomato Sauce (page 165)

2 cups shredded mozzarella

1. Peel, salt, and rinse the eggplant if desired (see note on page 113). Season the eggplant and zucchini well with salt and pepper. Heat 2 tablespoons of oil in a sauté pan over medium-high heat. Working in batches, add the sliced eggplant and zucchini and cook until lightly browned on both sides, about 10 minutes. Repeat, adding more oil to the pan as necessary, until all of the eggplant and zucchini is prepared. Set aside.

2. Add the mushrooms to the pan and sauté until the moisture they release has cooked away; add 1 teaspoon pepper, the garlic powder, and half the Parmesan cheese. Set aside.

3. In a small bowl, blend the ricotta, eggs, and parsley until smooth. Keep refrigerated until needed.

4. When you are ready to begin assembling the lasagna, put the lasagna noodles into a deep pan containing warm salted water and let them soften for about 10 minutes.

5. To assemble the lasagna, spread a thin layer of the tomato sauce, followed by a layer of lasagna noodles, then half of the ricotta mixture, followed by a layer of zucchini, eggplant, and mushrooms. Sprinkle with half of the remaining Parmesan and then half of the mozzarella. Repeat the same sequence of sauce, noodles, ricotta, vegetables, and cheese until the pan is filled. End with a layer of noodles. Press down on the lasagna gently to press out any pockets of air. Cover the noodles with enough tomato sauce to keep them from drying out as the lasagna bakes. (If the lasagna is prepared ahead, you can stop at this point, cover the pan carefully and keep it in the refrigerator for up to 24 hours.)

6. Preheat the oven to 325 degrees F. Cover the lasagna pan with foil and bake until the lasagna noodles are fully cooked, 45 minutes to 1 hour. Remove the foil, sprinkle with shredded mozzarella to cover top, and continue to bake until the cheese has melted and is slightly browned, 15 to 20 minutes. Let the lasagna rest for 15 minutes before cutting. Serve on heated plates.

eggplant parmesan

THIS EGGPLANT recipe includes a creamy ricotta layer for a moist dish with a lighter texture than a typical eggplant Parmesan. Assemble individual servings in ovenproof gratin dishes, if you wish.

MAKES 8 SERVINGS

1¼ lb sliced eggplant (about 1 large or 2 medium)

1½ cups ricotta cheese

1 cup grated Parmesan

½ cup minced flat-leaf parsley

Freshly grated nutmeg as needed, optional

Salt as needed

Freshly ground black pepper as needed

4 large eggs

⅔ cup milk

2 cups flour

2 cups dry bread crumbs, or as needed

4 cups canola oil, use as needed

3 cups Tomato Sauce (page 165), heated

2 cups grated mozzarella cheese

1. Peel, salt, and rinse the eggplant if desired (see "Preparing Eggplant for Cooking" on page 113).

2. Blend the ricotta, ½ cup Parmesan, the parsley, nutmeg, if using, ½ teaspoon salt, ¼ teaspoon pepper, and 1 egg until smooth. Keep refrigerated until needed.

2. Blend the remaining 3 eggs with the milk in a shallow bowl to make an egg wash. Put the flour in a second shallow bowl and season with a pinch of salt and pepper. Put the bread crumbs in a third shallow bowl.

3. Dip the eggplant slices one at a time into the flour, then the egg wash, and last, the bread crumbs, patting the crumbs evenly over all sides of the eggplant. Transfer the eggplant slices to a plate or baking sheet.

4. Pour about ½ inch of oil into a deep skillet and heat over medium high heat until the oil shimmers. Add the breaded eggplant slices to the hot oil, a few pieces at a time, and fry on the first side until golden brown, about 2 minutes. Turn the eggplant and continue to fry until golden and crisp on the second side, 2 minutes. Transfer to a plate lined with paper towels; continue until all of the eggplant is fried.

5. Preheat the oven to 350 degrees F.

6. Spread some of the tomato sauce in a lasagna pan, rectangular baking dish, or individual casseroles. Assemble the dish in layers: a layer of fried eggplant, a layer of the ricotta mixture, another layer of eggplant, topped with more tomato sauce. Sprinkle the assembled dish evenly with the mozzarella and the remaining Parmesan.

7. Cover the eggplant and bake until the ricotta mixture is very hot and the mozzarella cheese has melted, 20 to 25 minutes. Remove the cover and continue to bake until the cheese is golden brown, another 10 minutes. Let the dish rest for 10 minutes before cutting and serving.

orecchiette

with Peas, Mushrooms, Tomatoes, Ham, and Pecorino

ORECCHIETTE ARE little ear-shaped pastas, whose broad surfaces are perfect to pair with a chunky "sauce" of vegetables, ham, and cheese.

MAKES 6 SERVINGS

4 cups dry orecchiette pasta

2 tbsp butter

1 tbsp minced shallots

3 cups quartered or sliced white mushrooms

Salt as needed

Freshly ground black pepper as needed

6 oz Smithfield ham, cut into julienne

3 fresh or canned plum tomatoes, peeled, seeded, and chopped

1½ cups green peas (thawed if frozen)

2 cups heavy cream

3 tbsp chopped sage

½ cup pecorino Romano cheese

3 tbsp chopped flat-leaf parsley

1. Bring a large pot of water to a rolling boil. Salt generously (the water should taste noticeably salty). Add the orecchiette, stir once or twice, and cook until tender to the bite, about 8 minutes. Drain well and keep hot.

2. Heat the butter in the pasta pot over medium heat until it stops foaming. Add the shallots and cook, stirring frequently, until tender and limp, about 2 minutes. Add the mushrooms and continue to sauté, stirring frequently, until the mushrooms are tender and cooked through, about 5 minutes. Season the mushrooms with salt and pepper to taste.

3. Add the ham, tomatoes, peas, and cream to the pan and bring to a simmer. Cook over low heat, stirring from time to time, until the sauce has a good consistency and flavor, about 3 minutes. Add the sage and half of the Romano cheese. Stir well and adjust the seasoning to taste with salt and pepper if necessary.

4. Return the cooked orecchiette to pot and gently stir and toss to coat the pasta. Serve the pasta at once in heated bowls topped with the remaining Romano cheese and the parsley.

spicy bucatini with mussels and clams

Bucatini Arrabiata con Cozze e Vongole

*P*IERCED SPAGHETTI, called *bucatini*, looks like fatter-than-usual spaghetti. Its hollow center lets sauce coat the pasta on the inside and outside for even more flavor. If you can't find pierced spaghetti, linguini or fettuccini is good, too.

MAKES 8 SERVINGS

3 tbsp extra-virgin olive oil

1 cup minced yellow onion

8 garlic cloves, sliced thin

1 tsp red pepper flakes

6 cups finely chopped plum tomatoes, peeled and seeded

½ cup basil chiffonade

¼ cup chopped flat-leaf parsley

Salt as needed

Freshly ground black pepper as needed

2 lb dry bucatini pasta

2 dozen mussels, rinsed, debearded (see note)

2 dozen littleneck clams, rinsed

1. Heat the oil in a skillet over large saucepot. Add the onion and cook until tender and limp, about 5 minutes. Add the garlic and continue to sauté, stirring frequently, until aromatic, another 2 minutes. Add the red pepper flakes and cook over low heat until very flavorful, about 5 minutes.

2. Add the tomatoes to the pan and bring to a slow simmer. Cook over low heat, stirring from time to time, until the sauce has a good consistency and flavor, about 20 minutes. Add the basil, parsley, salt, and pepper to taste.

3. Bring a large pot of water to a rolling boil while the sauce simmers. Salt generously (the water should taste noticeably salty). Add the pasta and cook until tender to the bite, about 8 minutes. Drain well and keep hot.

4. Add the mussels and clams to the sauce. Cover the pot and simmer until the mussels and clams open, about 10 minutes. Discard any that remain closed.

5. Return the cooked pasta to the pot and gently stir and toss to coat the pasta. Serve the pasta at once in heated bowls topped with clams, mussels, and additional sauce.

COOKING MUSSELS AND CLAMS

Mussels and clams are both delicious and attractive. They are best when you give them appropriate care. Remember that they should be alive when you buy them and when they go into the pot. The first, and most important, step is buying them from a reliable source. The fish market, stall, or counter you visit should smell pleasantly of the sea and be very busy. Strong or unpleasant odors may be sign that the fish is not fresh. The faster the fish is sold, the fresher it is likely to be.

Keep clams and mussels in paper bags or wrapping in the refrigerator until you are ready to cook them. Try to buy seafood the day you want to cook it, but if you need to hold it for a day or two, it will be fine.

When you are ready to cook mussels and clams, the first step is to clean them well. Put them in a colander, set them in the sink, and turn on the cold water tap. One by one, take the shellfish in one hand and a scrub brush in the other. Clean the shells thoroughly under running cold water. You may see that some of the shellfish has opened up. As long as the shell snaps shut again when you tap it, the mussel or clam is fine. If it stays open, throw it out.

Mussels require an extra step to clean them. Trap the hairy "beard" between the flat side of a paring knife blade and the pad of your thumb, then tug and pull the beard away.

Once the clams and mussels are cooked, the shells will open up and the edges of the meat inside should be curled. If any of them do not open, that is a sign that they were not alive. Don't serve unopened cooked shellfish; throw it out.

rolled pasta with mushroom sauce

Rotolo

STANDARD WHITE mushrooms make a wonderful sauce, but if you can find exotic varieties, try substituting them for some of the white mushrooms. If you use a variety, be sure that you have a total of 4 cups of sliced mushrooms.

MAKES 8 SERVINGS

MUSHROOM SAUCE

¼ cup olive oil

¾ cup minced onion

4 cups sliced white mushrooms

1 cup dry red wine

2 cups diced plum tomatoes

2 tbsp minced marjoram leaves

1 tsp minced thyme leaves

Salt as needed

Freshly ground black pepper as needed

16 dry lasagna noodles

2 cups whole or part-skim ricotta cheese

1 cup grated Parmesan cheese

2 cups grated Fontina

½ lb thinly sliced prosciutto

1. To make the mushroom sauce: Heat the olive oil in a skillet over medium-high heat. Add the onion and sauté, stirring frequently, until the onion is translucent and tender, 10 to 12 minutes. Add the mushrooms and continue to sauté, stirring frequently, until the mushrooms are tender, another 8 to 10 minutes. Add the wine and cook over high heat until the wine is reduced by half. Add the tomatoes and herbs, reduce the heat slightly, and simmer until the sauce has a good consistency, about 15 minutes. Season to taste with salt and pepper.

2. While the sauce is simmering, cook the lasagna noodles in boiling salted water until tender, about 12 minutes. Drain the noodles thoroughly and rinse in cold water. Drain again.

3. Preheat the oven to 400 degrees F.

4. Combine the ricotta and parmesan cheeses, and season to taste with salt and pepper. Lay one noodle flat on a work surface and spread the noodle with 2 tablespoons of the ricotta mixture. Scatter about a tablespoon of the Fontina over the ricotta and top with a slice of prosciutto. Roll up the pasta and lay it seam-side down in a baking dish. Repeat until all of the noodles are filled and rolled.

5. Ladle the mushroom sauce over the noodles and bake the pasta until very hot and bubbly, about 30 minutes. Let the pasta rolls rest for 10 minutes before serving.

"straw and hay" fettuccini

with Smoked Salmon, Dill, and Mushrooms

STRAW AND hay refers to the blend of egg and wheat pastas. The egg pasta is straw and the wheat pasta is hay. If you make this dish in the spring, be sure to include fresh asparagus tips and replace the white mushrooms with the ultimate springtime delicacy—morels.

MAKES 6 SERVINGS

½ lb whole wheat fettuccini

½ lb egg fettuccini

3 tbsp olive oil

1 tbsp minced shallots

6 garlic cloves, sliced thin

2 cups white mushrooms, quartered

Salt as needed

Freshly ground black pepper as needed

1 cup dry white wine

2 cups heavy cream

1 cup green peas (thawed if frozen)

6 slices smoked salmon, cut into thin slivers

½ bunch dill, chopped

4 scallions, split and sliced ½-inch-thick on a diagonal

1. Bring a large pot of water to a rolling boil. Salt generously (the water should taste noticeably salty). Add the whole wheat fettuccini to the pot and stir once or twice; return the water to a boil and continue to boil for 2 minutes. Add the egg fettuccini and stir until the strands are all softened and separate. Continue to cook both types of fettuccini until they are tender to the bite, about 8 minutes. Drain well and keep hot.

2. While the pasta is cooking, heat the olive oil in a deep skillet over medium heat. Add the shallots and cook, stirring frequently, until tender and limp, about 2 minutes. Add the garlic and sauté until aromatic, another minute. Add the mushrooms and continue to sauté, stirring frequently, until the mushrooms are tender and cooked through, about 5 minutes. Season the mushrooms with salt and pepper to taste.

3. Add the white wine to the skillet and bring to a rapid simmer. Continue to simmer until ¾ of the wine has cooked away. Add the heavy cream and simmer the sauce until lightly thickened, 3 to 4 minutes. Add the peas, salmon, and dill. Simmer until all ingredients are very hot and the sauce is flavorful, about 2 minutes.

4. Add the fettuccini to the sauce and gently stir and toss to coat the pasta. Serve the pasta at once in heated bowls topped with the sliced scallions.

bacon and gruyère quiche

THIS SIMPLE quiche is rich and delicious. To create your own quiche, try other cheeses or even a blend of cheeses. Replace the bacon with diced ham or prosciutto, or try adding some sautéed domestic or exotic mushrooms.

MAKES 6 SERVINGS

1 tbsp butter

1 cup minced onion

3 large eggs

1½ cups heavy cream

½ tsp salt

¼ tsp freshly ground black pepper

¾ cup grated Gruyère cheese

8 slices bacon, cooked and crumbled

One 9-inch pie crust, prebaked

1. Preheat the oven to 350 degrees F.

2. Heat the butter in a sauté pan over medium heat. Add the onion and sauté until golden, about 8 minutes. Remove and reserve.

3. Combine the eggs, heavy cream, salt, and pepper in a mixing bowl and whisk until evenly blended. Stir the cheese, bacon, and reserved onion into the egg mixture. Spread the egg mixture evenly in the pie crust.

4. Set the quiche on a baking sheet and bake until a knife blade inserted in the center comes out clean, 40 to 45 minutes. If the pie crust begins to over brown, cover the edges of the pie crust with strips of aluminum foil or pie shields. Remove the quiche from the oven and cool on a wire rack. Let the quiche rest at least 20 minutes before cutting. Serve hot, warm, or room temperature.

macaroni timbale

THE SHAPE and size of the dish you choose for the timbale will have a direct impact on how dramatic it looks once you unmold it. Large soufflé dishes are good or you can use a springform pan to make it easy to get the timbale out of the pan and onto a serving platter.

MAKES 8 SERVINGS

1 cup Arborio or other round-grain rice

4 large eggs, lightly beaten

2½ cups grated Parmesan

¼ cup olive oil

½ cup minced onion

1 cup sliced cremini mushrooms

1 lb ground turkey

2 tbsp tomato paste

Two 28-ounce cans whole tomatoes, pureed through a food mill

Salt as needed

Freshly ground black pepper as needed

2 tsp sugar

Few grains freshly grated nutmeg

3 sprigs fresh basil, leaves only, minced

2 cups dry ziti or penne pasta

1 cup green peas (thawed if frozen)

¼ cup plain bread crumbs

Egg wash of 1 egg beaten with 1 tbsp milk

1. To prepare the rice, bring a large pot of salted water to a rolling boil. Add the rice in a thin stream and stir it with a fork to prevent the rice from clumping. Continue to simmer the rice until tender, 15 to 16 minutes. Drain the rice through a fine-mesh sieve and spread it out in a thin layer in a baking dish to cool it quickly. When the rice has cooled to room temperature, transfer it to a bowl and, using a wooden spoon, stir in the eggs and 2 cups grated Parmesan. Place it in the refrigerator to chill and firm (this will take several hours or overnight).

2. To prepare the mushroom-tomato sauce: Heat the olive oil in a sauce pan over medium heat. Add the onion and cook, stirring frequently, until the onion is golden, 12 to 15 minutes. Add the mushrooms and increase the heat to medium-high. Sauté the mushrooms, stirring frequently, until the liquid they release cooks away, 6 to 8 minutes. Add the ground turkey and cook the meat over medium heat, stirring frequently, until the meat is cooked and has lost its raw appearance, about 5 minutes. Add the tomato paste and sauté for another minute before adding the pureed tomatoes. Bring the sauce to a simmer and continue to cook until the sauce is a good consistency and flavor, about 45 minutes. Season to taste with salt, pepper, sugar, and nutmeg. Stir in the basil and remove the sauce from the heat. Strain the sauce through a colander, catching the liquid in a bowl while allowing the solids to remain in the colander.

3. While the sauce is simmering, cook the pasta in boiling salted water according to the package directions. Be sure to slightly undercook the pasta, as it will continue to cook as the timbale bakes. Drain the pasta well and mix it with a little of the strained sauce; use only enough to barely coat the pasta. Add most of the reserved solids from the colander and stir in the peas and ½ cup grated Parmesan. (Reserve the strained sauce to serve with the sliced timbale at the table.)

4. Preheat the oven to 400°F

5. To assemble the timbale, brush a 5-quart ovenproof casserole with butter and coat it with bread crumbs. Press a generous ¾ of the chilled rice mixture into the bowl, making a lining that is ½ inch thick. Fill the lined bowl with the pasta

mixture and finish enclosing the timbale with more of the rice mixture, spread in an even layer over the pasta. Seal the rim of the timbale well and brush it with the egg wash.

6. Place the timbale on a rack in the center of the oven. Bake until the rice is a rich golden brown color, about 1 hour. Re-move the timbale from the oven and, using a small knife, gently loosen the timbale from the bowl. Let the timbale rest for about 15 minutes before inverting it onto a serving platter. Cut into wedges and serve with tomato sauce, grated cheese, and freshly ground black pepper.

frittata with bacon, corn and pasta

FRITTATAS ARE traditional Italian open-face omelets perfect for a simple family supper. They are an excellent way to use any leftovers you may have from the night before: cooked pasta or potatoes, cooked vegetables, or a small piece of cheese. If you are adding cooked ingredients, put them in the pan and let them warm over low heat before you add the beaten eggs. Since your leftovers were most likely already sea-soned, be sure to take that into account when you season the beaten eggs.

MAKES 4 SERVINGS

1 tbsp butter

4 strips bacon, diced

2 cups corn kernels, cooked

1 bunch scallions, minced

½ jalapeño, diced, optional

2 cups cooked spaghetti

½ cup chopped flat-leaf parsley

Salt as needed

Freshly ground black pepper as needed

8 large eggs, beaten

1 cup grated dry-aged Jack cheese

1. Preheat the broiler to high. Position a rack about 3 or 4 inches from the heat source.

2. Heat an ovenproof sauté pan over medium heat, add the butter and melt. Add the bacon and cook until the bacon is al-most crisp, 3 to 4 minutes.

3. Add the cooked corn kernels, scallions, and the jalapeño, if using, and cook an additional 3 to 4 minutes, being careful not to brown the corn.

4. Add the cooked pasta and the parsley. Season to taste with salt and pepper.

5. Add the eggs and stir vigorously until the eggs are warm but still liquid. Top with grated cheese, and transfer the frittata to the preheated broiler, cooking until the eggs are set and the top just begins to brown, 2 to 3 minutes.

6. Allow the frittata to cool slightly then transfer to a serv-ing platter and divide into portions.

macaroni and cheese

Pasta Quattro Formaggi

Four cheeses combine in this dish for a complex flavor. We've chosen fusilli pasta instead of ordinary elbows, but any short pierced pasta shape will be good.

MAKES 6 SERVINGS

2¾ cups heavy cream

1 cup Emmenthaler cheese

1 cup Gruyère cheese

1 cup Danish blue (Danablu) cheese

¾ cup grated Parmesan

1¼ pounds fusilli (corkscrew pasta)

2 tsp freshly ground black pepper, or to taste

1. Preheat the oven to 350 degrees F. Bring a large pot of well salted water to a boil for the pasta.

2. Pour the cream into a large saucepan and place it over medium heat, watching carefully to avoid scorching. Bring the cream to a simmer and reduce it by ¼, about 5 minutes. Reduce the heat to low and add the cheeses, stirring occasionally while the cheese melts, about 10 minutes.

3. While the cheese is melting, cook the pasta until it is tender to the bite, about 8 to 10 minutes. Drain well.

4. Add the cooked pasta to the cream sauce mixture, toss to coat, and season with pepper. (Salt should not be needed due to the saltiness of the water used for cooking the pasta and the saltiness of the cheese.)

5. Transfer to a greased casserole dish or baking pan. Bake until the macaroni and cheese is hot and creamy and a golden crust has formed on the top, about 20 minutes.

shepherd's pie

Shepherd's pie is a great way to use up a traditional Sunday roast. If you have cooked meats on hand, substitute diced or shredded cooked meat for the ground meat we've used here. Even better, if you have the pan drippings or gravy, use the drippings to replace some or all of the tomato sauce.

MAKES 6 SERVINGS

2 tbsp olive oil

1½ lb lean ground beef or turkey

1 cup minced onion

½ cup minced celery

1 cup diced carrot

1 cup green peas (thawed if frozen)

1 cup green beans

1½ cups Tomato Sauce (page 165)

3 tbsp tomato paste

½ cup dry red wine, optional

Salt as needed

Freshly ground black pepper as needed

2 tbsp chopped flat-leaf parsley

1 tbsp chopped oregano or thyme

3 cups mashed potatoes (see note)

1. Heat the oil in a large skillet over medium heat until it shimmers. Crumble the ground beef or turkey into the pan and sauté, stirring frequently, until the meat no longer looks raw, about 5 minutes. Add the onion, celery, carrot, peas, and green beans. Reduce the heat to low and cook, stirring frequently, until the onion is translucent and all of the vegetables are hot, 8 to 10 minutes. Add the tomato sauce, tomato paste, and wine, if using, and bring to a simmer. Season to taste with salt and pepper. Simmer, stirring from time to time, until the sauce has thickened, 10 to 12 minutes. Remove the skillet from the heat and stir in the parsley and oregano or thyme.

2. Preheat the oven to 350 degrees F.

3. Transfer the meat mixture to a 2½ quart casserole. Spoon or pipe the potatoes into an even layer that completely covers the meat. Bake until the potatoes are very hot with a light golden crust, about 30 minutes. Serve immediately.

MASHED POTATOES

Hot freshly mashed potatoes make the lightest topping for a shepherd's pie, but you certainly can use potatoes that you cooked and mashed ahead of time. To make mashed potatoes to use as a topping here or to serve as an accompaniment to braised dishes with rich gravies like lamb shanks (page 82), follow these guidelines:

Plan on about four medium potatoes for six servings. Scrub them well, peel, and cut into chunks of a roughly even size. Put them into a pan with enough cold water to cover them by an inch or two.

Add salt to the water; use enough to give the water a noticeably salty taste. Bring the water to a boil over high heat, and then reduce the heat until the water is simmering. Keep the water at a simmer until you can pierce the potatoes easily with a skewer or fork, about 15 minutes, depending on the size of your chunks.

Drain the potatoes in colander. An optional step, but one that is worth the trouble, is to put the cooked potatoes back into the pot. Return the pot to low heat and let the potatoes steam dry for a few minutes.

Use a potato masher, food mill, or potato rice to puree the potatoes. You can use a hand mixer or a stand mixer with a paddle if you are making a lot of potatoes. Stir in 1 or 2 tablespoons of warm milk for every potato you cooked. Season the potatoes with salt and pepper and stir in butter or fresh herbs, if you like.

potato casserole with parsnips and leeks

ANY EASTERN European cuisines feature a potato casserole similar to this one. Whether the kugel of Lithuania, made with cream instead of broth and typically cooked with bacon fat rather than schmaltz of the Ashkenazi Jews, this dish deserves to take a starring role at the table for a simple but hearty dinner. Try it baked in a cast iron skillet for the best crust. Cut it into wedges and serve topped with sour cream and a side dish of vinegared cucumbers.

MAKES 6 TO 8 SERVINGS

6 yellow potatoes, peeled and cut into large dice

3 parsnips, peeled and cut into large dice

¼ cup rendered schmaltz (see note)

1 onion, grated

1 leek, white part only, cut into small dice

3 large eggs, beaten

½ cup matzo meal

½ cup chicken broth or water

1 tsp baking powder

Salt as needed

Freshly ground pepper as needed

Pinch freshly grated nutmeg

1. Cook the potatoes and parsnips separately in salted boiling water until they are tender, 10 to 12 minutes. Drain thoroughly and combine in a large bowl. Using a ricer or potato masher, rice or mash the potatoes and parsnips until they form a smooth purée.

2. Preheat the oven to 350 degrees F. Heat the chicken fat in a medium sauté pan over medium heat until it shimmers. Add the onion and leek and sauté, stirring frequently, until lightly browned, 8 to 10 minutes. Transfer to a plate and let cool completely.

3. Add the onion mixture to the vegetables. Add the eggs, matzo meal, broth or water, and baking powder, and blend well. Add salt, pepper, and nutmeg to taste. Transfer the mixture into a well-greased 8-inch square baking dish. Bake until the top is nicely browned, about 20 to 30 minutes. Serve hot.

SCHMALTZ

Chicken fat (schmaltz) may be purchased (look for it in your dairy case), or you can reserve it from your homemade chicken broth. Once you've finished simmering and straining the broth, let it cool to at least 70 degrees F before putting it into the refrigerator. After the fat has hardened, lift the solid fat from the broth. You can melt the schmaltz to cook away any broth that remains, then store it in clean, covered jars in the refrigerator.

green enchiladas

Enchiladas Verdes

a GREEN ENCHILADA, stuffed with chicken and farmer's cheese, is a meal that's quick to assemble and bake. The fresh cilantro and mint give the sauce exceptional brightness, a perfect counterpoint to the rich and creamy filling.

MAKES 6 SERVINGS

2 teaspoons corn or olive oil

1 onion, medium dice

1 garlic clove, finely minced

1 cup farmer's or pot cheese

⅓ cup heavy cream

2 cups shredded or diced cooked chicken meat

3 tablespoons sliced almonds, toasted

2 cups quartered tomatillos

1 cup sliced scallions

⅔ cup chopped fresh cilantro

2 whole roasted jalapeños, seeded, diced

2 tablespoons chopped fresh mint

½ teaspoon ground cumin seed

½ teaspoon ground coriander seed

12 corn tortillas

6 oz Monterey Jack cheese, coarsely shredded

1. Preheat the oven to 350 degrees.

2. Heat the oil in a small skillet over medium heat until it shimmers. Add the onion and garlic, and sauté until the onion is a light golden brown, about 6 to 8 minutes. Remove the onion from the heat, spread it in a thin layer on a plate, and allow to cool completely.

3. Puree the farmer's cheese in a food processor until smooth. With the machine running, add the heavy cream in a stream. Remove the cheese mixture from the processor to a bowl. Fold in the chicken, almonds, and sautéed onion. Keep the filling in the refrigerator until ready to fill the enchiladas.

4. Place the tomatillos, scallions, cilantro, jalapeños, mint, cumin, and coriander in the food processor or blender and puree to form a sauce. Place the sauce in a shallow bowl.

5. Heat a cast iron skillet or other heavy-bottomed skillet over medium heat until quite hot. Soften the tortillas one at a time by toasting in the skillet for about 15 seconds on each side. Immediately dip the tortilla into the sauce to coat it very lightly and then set it on a work surface. Place a spoonful of the filling slightly to one side of the center of the tortilla and roll up into a cylinder. Place the filled and rolled enchilada in a buttered or oiled baking dish. Repeat with the remaining tortillas until all have been filled and rolled. Spoon the remaining sauce over the enchiladas.

6. Sprinkle the cheese over the enchiladas, cover the pan, and bake until the filling is hot, about 15 minutes. Remove the cover and bake long enough for the cheese topping to melt. Let the enchiladas rest for 5 minutes before serving on heated plates.

chicken pot pie

Use either white or light meat, or a combination of both, in this pot pie. Top your pot pie with pie crust, as we've done here, or substitute two sheets of puff pastry for a more dramatic presentation. Another option is a layer of your favorite biscuit dough (whether scratch, from a mix, or purchased), dolloped onto the filling just before the pot pie goes into the oven.

MAKES 4 TO 6 SERVINGS

3 tbsp butter or vegetable oil

1½ cups diced yellow onion

2 tsp minced garlic

3 tbsp flour

3 cups chicken broth

Salt as needed

Freshly ground black pepper as needed

1 cup diced carrot

1 cup diced celery

2 cups diced red or Yukon Gold potato

4 cups diced cooked chicken meat

1 cup green peas (thawed if frozen)

2 tbsp chopped flat-leaf parsley

Two 9-inch prepared pie crusts or puff pastry sheets

1. Preheat the oven to 350 degrees F.

2. Heat the butter or oil in a saucepan over medium-high heat until it shimmers. Add the onion and sauté, stirring frequently, until tender, 10 to 12 minutes. Add the garlic and sauté until aromatic, about 30 seconds. Add the flour and cook, stirring constantly, until pasty and thick, about 2 minutes. Add the broth, whisking well to work out any lumps. Bring to boil and then immediately reduce the heat to low and simmer, stirring frequently, until thick, about 15 minutes. Season to taste with salt and pepper.

3. Add the carrot, celery, and potato, and simmer until the vegetables are tender, about 20 minutes. Add the chicken and peas and remove from the heat. Season to taste with salt and pepper. Stir in the chopped parsley.

4. Spoon the filling into individual crocks or a baking dish. Cut pie crust or puff pastry dough to the appropriate size and shape and cover the filling. Cut vents in the crust and press the edges of the dough onto the baking dish or crocks to seal.

5. Bake the pot pie until the pie crust or puff pastry is golden and flaky, about 45 minutes for a large pot pie and 25 minutes for individual crocks. Serve immediately.

cassoulet

Cassoulet is a robust meal, filled with cured and smoked meats and sausages, baked in a stew of beans until a rich crust forms. According to tradition, the cook repeatedly breaks the crust and pushes it down into the stew.

MAKES 12 SERVINGS

12 cups chicken broth

3 cups dry navy beans, presoaked

1 lb slab bacon, sliced ¼ inch thick

1 lb garlic sausage

2 small yellow onions, peeled and left whole

3 garlic cloves

2 bouquets garnis (see page 57)

Salt as needed

1½ lb boneless pork loin, cut into large cubes

1½ lb boneless lamb shoulder or leg, cut into large cubes

Freshly ground black pepper as needed

6 tbsp olive oil

1 cup diced leeks

1 cup sliced carrots

1 cup sliced parsnips

1 tsp minced garlic

¼ cup all-purpose flour

⅓ cup dry white wine

6 cups beef broth

1 cup chopped plum tomatoes

1¾ lb duck confit

1½ cups bread crumbs

2 tbsp chopped flat-leaf parsley

1. Bring the chicken broth to a boil in a large saucepot and add the beans and bacon. Return the mixture to a simmer and cook, stirring occasionally, until the beans are nearly tender, about 40 minutes.

2. Add the sausage, onions, garlic, and 1 bouquet garni. Return the mixture to a simmer and cook until the sausage is cooked through and the bacon is fork tender, about 30 minutes. Remove and reserve the sausage and bacon. Remove and discard the onions, garlic, and bouquet garni.

3. Season the beans with salt to taste continue to simmer until the beans are tender, about 20 to 25 minutes. Strain the beans, reserve them, and return the cooking liquid to the pot. Continue to simmer until the liquid reduces by ½ and is beginning to thicken, about 30 minutes. Reserve the sauce for later use.

4. Season the pork and lamb with salt and pepper. Heat the oil in a casserole or Dutch oven over medium-high heat until it starts to shimmer. Sear the pork and lamb in the oil on all sides, turning as necessary, until deep brown. Transfer the meat to a pan and keep warm.

5. Add the leeks, carrots, and parsnips to the casserole and sauté, stirring occasionally, until the leeks are golden brown, about 15 minutes. Add the garlic and cook until aromatic, about 1 minute. Add the flour and cook, stirring frequently, until the mixture is pasty, about 5 minutes.

6. Add the wine and 3 cups of broth to the casserole, whisking or stirring until smooth. Stir in the tomatoes and the remaining bouquet garni. Return the seared meats to the casserole, along with any juices they may have released. Add more broth if necessary to keep the meat completely moistened. Bring to a slow simmer over medium-low heat.

7. Preheat the oven to 350 degrees F. Cover the casserole and braise the meat in the oven, skimming the surface as necessary, until the meats are fork tender, about 1 hour. *(recipe continues on page 136)*

8. Peel the reserved sausage and slice it ¼ inch thick. Slice the reserved bacon ¼ inch thick. Add the sliced sausage and bacon to the casserole. Cover the meat with a layer of the reserved beans. Add the duck confit in a layer, topped with the second half of the beans. Pour the sauce from the beans over the cassoulet. Toss together the bread crumbs and parsley and sprinkle in an even layer over the cassoulet.

9. Turn the oven down to 300 degrees F and bake the cassoulet, uncovered, periodically basting the crust with the juices that bubble up at the sides of the casserole, until it is heated through and a good crust has formed, 1½ to 2 hours. Let the cassoulet rest for 15 minutes before serving. Serve in heated bowls.

swordfish with a tomato-olive ragù

Pesce Spada Siciliana

YOU CAN replace the swordfish in this recipe with any firm, meaty fish you like. Halibut, cod, bass, or tuna are all good substitutes.

MAKES 6 SERVINGS

TOMATO-OLIVE RAGÙ

⅓ cup olive oil

1 cup minced onion

3 garlic cloves, minced to a paste

3 tbsp chopped capers

6 anchovy fillets

3 pints cherry tomatoes, hulled and halved or quartered if necessary

1 cup olives stuffed with chiles

3 tbsp chopped oregano leaves

Salt as needed

Freshly ground black pepper to taste as needed

6 swordfish steaks (about 6 oz each)

Juice of 2 lemons

⅔ cup sliced almonds, toasted

1. Preheat the oven to 400 degrees F.

2. To make the tomato olive ragù: Heat the oil in an ovenproof skillet over medium heat. Add the onion, garlic, capers, and anchovies to the pan and sauté, stirring frequently, until the onion is a very light golden brown, about 8 to 10 minutes. Add the tomatoes and continue to sauté, stirring or tossing frequently, until the tomatoes are very soft and all of the ingredients are very hot. Add the olives and oregano to the pan and continue to sauté for another 2 to 3 minutes. Season to taste with salt and pepper.

3. Cut 6 squares of foil large enough to hold the swordfish steaks. Place a spoonful of the tomato-olive ragù in the center of each piece of foil, top with a piece of swordfish, and then top with a little lemon juice and sliced almonds. Fold the foil around the fish to make a tight seal (the seams should be on the top of the packet).

4. Place the swordfish steaks in a shallow pan and bake until the fish is cooked through, about 12 minutes. Serve the fish directly from the foil.

persian molded rice with crisp potatoes

Chelou

THIS MAGNIFICENT dish is traditionally unmolded before it is served and then cut open at the table to make the most of its attractive crust of thinly sliced potatoes. This is a dish meant for a special occasion or celebration.

MAKES 6 SERVINGS

2 cups basmati rice

1 Yukon Gold potato

1 tsp saffron threads

½ cup milk

2 tbsp olive oil or clarified butter (see note)

Salt as needed

2 tbsp butter, melted

1. Preheat the oven to 350 degrees F. Rinse the basmati rice thoroughly in cold water. Put the rice in a bowl, add enough cold water to cover by 2 inches, and soak for 30 minutes.

2. While the rice is soaking, peel the potato and slice it as thinly as possible. Put the slices into a colander and rinse under cold running water to remove the starch from the surface of the potatoes. Blot the potatoes dry.

3. Bring a large pot of water to a rolling boil. Salt generously (the water should taste noticeably salty). Add the rice, stir once or twice, and cook exactly 6 minutes. Drain in sieve and set aside.

4. Meanwhile, in a dry skillet over medium heat, add the saffron to the pan and swirl it over the heat until the saffron is lightly toasted and aromatic, about 1 minute. Add the milk, immediately remove from the heat, and let the saffron steep in the milk while you continue with the recipe.

5. Heat the olive oil or clarified butter in a flameproof casserole or Dutch oven over medium heat until it shimmers. Remove the pan from the heat and carefully arrange the potato slices in a layer that covers the bottom of the casserole, overlapping the slices slightly. Season with salt.

6. Spread the rice in an even layer over the potatoes. Drizzle the saffron-infused milk and melted butter over the rice. Return the casserole to medium heat. When the potatoes are sizzling, cover the pan tightly with a lid or aluminum foil and place in oven until the potatoes are golden brown and crunchy, about 40 minutes. Loosen the rice from the sides of the pan and invert the chelou onto a warmed serving platter. Cut into wedges and serve immediately.

HOW TO CLARIFY BUTTER

Cut cold unsalted butter into pieces and put the pieces into a heavy saucepan. Melt over medium to low heat until the butter separates into layers; do not stir. Skim the foam from the butter and carefully ladle the clear butter into a clean container leaving the solids and milky liquid at the bottom of the pan.

sautés and stir-fries

SAUTÉS, STIR-FRIES, AND skillet meals are amazingly versatile. Some of these dishes are ready to serve in less than 15 minutes, once everything is chopped and measured. Some take a bit longer, so they are started in a skillet on top of the stove and then transferred to the oven to finish cooking.

The sautés we've included here are based on classic culinary technique: A tender, quick-cooking food is cooked very rapidly over brisk heat. The next step is to make a quick pan sauce that captures all the flavor and color that has collected in the bottom of the pan. To turn a classic sauté into a one dish meal, you might add vegetables to the pan. Very moist vegetables such as tomatoes or mushrooms can actually provide some of the moisture for your sauce. Add some shredded spinach or cabbage to introduce color and texture, or try adding some tender vegetables, or vegetables that you've already cooked: peas, corn, potatoes, or squashes. Just remember that if the vegetable goes into the pan raw, you'll either need to give it enough time to cook properly or cook it separately by steaming, boiling, or roasting.

Skillet dishes call for a skillet with an ovenproof handle. If you have the kind of cast iron skillet sometimes referred to as a chicken fryer, use it. The handle is metal, and the sides of the pan are just high enough to accommodate a generous helping of vegetables, beans, and other ingredients. Sauté pans or skillets with handles made from plastic or composite materials, however, usually can't go in a hot oven.

Woks or stir-fry pans are best for making stir-fries. Woks have rounded bottoms, so you may need to use a wok ring to keep it stable over the burner as you work. Stir-fry pans have curved sides like a wok, but a flat bottom to use on burners without a stand. The stir-fries you make at home may not have the exact same textures and colors as those you enjoy at your favorite restaurant. That is because in restaurants, the amount of heat under the wok is far greater than you could ever get from most home ranges. To be sure you are actually stir-frying, rather than stewing, don't overcrowd the wok or add too many ingredients at once. If your stir-fry looks too wet, push the ingredients up onto the sides of the wok and let the liquid in the bottom of the wok cook away.

vegetarian grandmother's bean curd

Su Ma Po Dofu

S NOW PEAS cook quickly in stir-fries, but to enjoy them at their best, they need to be prepared correctly. First, snap away the end that was attached to the vine, but don't pull it completely away. Pull the end down toward the tip so that you pull the coarse string on the side of the snow pea away.

MAKES 4 SERVINGS

1¼ lb firm tofu

¼ cup canola or peanut oil

2 tbsp thinly sliced scallion

2 tsp minced ginger root

2 tsp minced garlic

2 tbsp black bean sauce

1 tbsp hot bean paste

1 tsp Korean chili powder, optional

1 cup sliced shiitake mushroom caps

1 cup snow peas, cut in half on the diagonal

1 medium red bell pepper, seeded and cut into strips

1 cup bean sprouts

2 tbsp vegetarian oyster sauce

1 tbsp sesame oil

2 tbsp minced cilantro

Salt as needed.

Ground white pepper as needed

½ tsp Szechwan peppercorn powder

Steamed white rice, optional (see page 160)

1. Press the tofu and cut it into triangles (see page 142) and blot dry. Heat the oil in a wok or deep skillet over high heat until nearly smoking. Add the tofu and fry, turning once or twice, until the tofu is light golden brown on all sides, about 5 minutes. Transfer the tofu to a rack or paper towel and let it drain well. Keep warm.

2. Pour out all but 2 tablespoons of the oil from the wok and return it to high heat. Add the scallions, ginger, and garlic. Stir-fry until aromatic, about 1 minute. Add the black bean sauce, hot bean paste, and chili powder, if using.

3. Add the mushroom caps, snow peas, red pepper, and bean sprouts. Continue to stir-fry until the vegetables are very hot, about 5 minutes.

4. Add the fried tofu, oyster sauce, sesame oil, cilantro, salt, and pepper. Stir-fry until all of the ingredients are very hot, another 3 minutes. Stir in the Szechwan peppercorn powder. Serve immediately on heated plates, accompanied with steamed rice if desired.

CLOCKWISE FROM UPPER LEFT Many Asian dishes use a combination of chopped ginger root, garlic, and scallions as a foundation for flavor. When deep frying tofu, don't crowd the pan with too many pieces, as it will bring down the temperature of the oil.; finished tofu should have a uniformly golden brown color. Before adding the tofu to the pan, stir-fry the vegetables until tender but still retaining their vibrant color. The finished Vegetarian Grandmother's Bean Curd is shown here accompanied by steamed white rice.

vegetarian stir-fried tofu and rice noodles

Pad Thai

SMOKED TOFU has a rich flavor that adds to this dish. It also has a firmer texture than regular tofu. If you can't locate smoked tofu, you can use firm tofu that you've pressed.

MAKES 4 SERVINGS

2 tbsp roasted chili paste (nahm prik pow)

4 tbsp light soy sauce

¼ cup rice wine vinegar

¼ cup palm sugar (see page 54)

2 tsp salt

1½ lb rice noodles, ¼-inch wide

¼ cup vegetable oil

1 lb smoked tofu, cut into sticks

1 leek, white and light-green portions, julienne

2 tbsp chopped garlic

3 large eggs, lightly beaten

2 scallions, sliced into thin 1-inch-long strips

2 cups vegetable or mushroom broth

½ lb bean sprouts

¼ cup roughly chopped cilantro

½ cup coarsely chopped pan-roasted peanuts (see page 44)

8 lime wedges

1. Whisk together the chili paste, soy sauce, rice wine vinegar, palm sugar, and salt to make a seasoning mixture. Set aside. Put the rice noodles in a bowl and add enough warm water to cover them. Let the noodles soften for 30 minutes, drain, and set aside.

2. Heat a wok over high heat, add 3 tablespoons of oil, and heat until nearly smoking. Add the tofu, leek, and garlic. Stir-fry until the leek brightens in color and softens slightly and the garlic is light gold, about 3 minutes.

3. Add the noodles and stir-fry until hot and coated with the oil. Push the noodles to the upper edge of one side of the wok. Add the remaining 1 tablespoon oil to the wok. Add the beaten eggs to the empty space in the wok. Fold the noodles over the eggs and let the mixture cook, undisturbed, for 20 seconds. Then, begin to stir-fry the noodle-egg mixture again.

4. Add the seasoning mixture and the scallions. Stir-fry until the noodles are soft, adding broth as necessary to moisten the noodles.

5. Fold in the sprouts and cilantro. Garnish with peanuts and lime wedges and serve at once on heated plates.

WORKING WITH TOFU

Tofu is sold in blocks that usually weigh about 12 ounces. It is packed in liquid to keep it fresh and to prevent it from drying out. Tofu is a perishable food that will be best if you prepare it within 2 days of purchase. Tofu is available in a variety of firmnesses: silk, which is very soft and slippery almost like a custard; medium, and firm. For tofu that you plan to sauté or stir-fry, buy firm tofu. You also can press the tofu to firm it up even more as follows:

Put 3 or 4 layers of paper towels in a plate or baking pan. Remove the tofu from the package and put it on the plate. Add 3 or 4 more layers of paper towels to cover the tofu. Next, put something flat, like a baking pan, on top of the stack. Set a few cans in the pan for weight. Put the whole assembly into the refrigerator and let the tofu drain for about 1 hour.

Many recipes call for the tofu to be cut into triangles. First, cut the block in half width-wise. Now cut the two large rectangles in half, cutting from one corner to its opposite on the diagonal.

spicy eggs and sweet peppers

eGG DISHES are popular in Tunisian cuisine. In this rendition, eggs are nestled into a "hash" of sweet and hot peppers and baked until the eggs have cooked through. Choose a good-quality, flavorful olive oil because it is such an important part of the dish.

MAKES 4 SERVINGS

½ cup extra-virgin olive oil

2 green bell peppers, peeled, seeded and chopped

2 jalapeños or other hot red or green chiles, seeded and chopped

¼ cup tomato paste

2 tbsp Harissa (recipe follows)

1 tbsp paprika

1 tbsp caraway seeds

2 cups water or as needed

Salt as needed

Freshly ground black pepper as needed

8 large eggs

1. Heat the olive oil in a large skillet over high heat until it shimmers. Add the bell peppers and jalapeños or chiles and sauté, stirring frequently, until the peppers are tender and have started to release their juices, about 2 minutes. Add the tomato paste and cook, stirring constantly, to a rich, sweet aroma, about 30 seconds. Add the harissa, paprika, and caraway seeds and stir until the mixture is evenly blended. Add enough water to make a loose, stew-like consistency. Season to taste with salt and pepper.

2. Bring the sauce to a boil, reduce the heat to low, and simmer until the sauce is very flavorful and the liquid has reduced and thickened, about 20 minutes.

3. Push the peppers aside to make 8 small "wells" and crack 1 egg into each well without breaking the yolks. Continue to cook, covered, over low heat until the eggs whites are firm and set, about 15 minutes. Serve the eggs and peppers directly from the skillet on heated plates.

Harissa

MAKES ½ CUP

4 ounces dried New Mexico chiles

2 tsp minced garlic

1 tsp fresh lemon juice

¾ tsp ground caraway

½ tsp ground coriander

1 tbsp olive oil

1. Remove the stem and seeds from the chiles and place in a bowl. Add enough cold water to cover them and let them soak for 15 minutes. When the chiles are softened, drain them well and press to remove any excess water. Chop the chiles coarsely.

2. Transfer the chiles to a food processor and puree with the garlic, lemon juice, caraway, and coriander to a fine paste. Add the olive oil through the feed tube with the machine running until completely incorporated. Transfer the harissa to a jar and hold, covered, under refrigeration until ready to serve.

stir-fried glass noodles

Jap Chae

*i*F YOU can locate Korean glass noodles, also known as dang myun, use them in this dish. They are similar to cellophane or glass noodles made from mung beans, but they are slightly thicker and chewier.

MAKES 4 SERVINGS

10 dried oak mushrooms

1 oz dried wood ear mushrooms

One 18-oz package glass noodles or Asian vermicelli

3 scallions, sliced thin

½ cup light soy sauce

1 tbsp dark sesame oil

2 tbsp sugar

½ cup vegetable oil

1 cup thinly sliced onion

1 tbsp minced garlic

1 cup red bell pepper julienne

2 cups shredded green cabbage

1 cup carrot julienne

Salt as needed

Freshly ground black pepper as needed

5 large eggs, lightly beaten

1. Rehydrate the oak mushrooms and wood ears separately in cool water (see page 91). Drain and reserve the soaking liquid to moisten the noodles if necessary. Cut off the stems and any hard portions of the mushrooms and discard them. Cut the caps into ⅛-inch wide strips. Set aside.

2. Pour enough boiling water over the noodles to cover them by at least 2 inches. Soak until rehydrated and elastic, about 15 minutes. Drain, rinse with cool water, and reserve.

3. Stir together the scallions, soy sauce, sesame oil, and sugar in a small bowl. Set aside.

4. Heat the oil in a wok or skillet over high heat until it shimmers. Add the onion and garlic and stir-fry until tender, about 2 minutes.

5. Add the red bell pepper, cabbage, carrot, and mushrooms. Stir-fry until the vegetables are very hot, about 5 minutes. Add the scallion-soy sauce mixture and stir-fry until all of the ingredients are evenly coated. Add the noodles and stir-fry until very hot, 4 to 5 minutes. Season with to taste with salt and pepper.

6. Pour the eggs over the noodles and vegetables and stir-fry until the eggs are thickened and set, another 3 minutes. Serve immediately on heated plates.

garden-style quinoa pilaf

Quinoa Jardinère

ONE OF the more ancient grains grown in the New World, quinoa (pronounced "KEEN-wah") is a light, fluffy grain with a subtle flavor. Any leftovers from this dish could be combined with additional diced vegetables such as cucumbers, carrots, celery, avocado, and tomato, and then dressed with a vinaigrette.

MAKES 6 SERVINGS

2 tsp canola oil

1 tbsp minced shallot

1 clove garlic, minced

2 cups chicken broth

⅔ cup quinoa, rinsed in several changes of cool water

1 small bay leaf

1 sprig fresh thyme or ½ tsp dried

Salt as needed

Freshly ground pepper as needed

2 tbsp butter

1 cup small-dice red bell pepper

1 cup small-dice green bell pepper

½ cup small-dice carrot

½ cup small-dice celery

3 tbsp minced jalapeño peppers

2 tsp minced ginger root

3 tbsp minced scallions

2 tbsp minced parsley

2 tbsp minced basil

1 tbsp minced thyme

1. Heat the oil in a saucepan over medium heat. Add the shallot and garlic and sauté until aromatic and tender, 2 to 3 minutes. Add the broth, quinoa, bay leaf, thyme, and ¼ teaspoon salt. Stir well with a fork, and bring the broth to a simmer over medium heat.

2. Cover the pot and simmer the quinoa over low heat (or in a 325°F oven) until tender and very fluffy, about 15 minutes.

3. Remove and discard the bay leaf and thyme sprig. Fluff the grains with a fork to break up any clumps. Season to taste with salt and pepper and set aside.

4. Heat the butter in the pot over medium heat until it stops foaming. Add the red and green peppers, carrot, celery, jalapeño, and ginger. Sauté stirring frequently until the peppers are tender, about 10 minutes. Season to taste with salt and pepper. Fold in the quinoa, scallions, parsley, basil, and thyme. Serve at once on heated plates.

stir-fried squid with basil

FRESH OR frozen squid is available already cleaned at many markets and fishmongers. All you need to do is cut the body into rings and chop the tentacles.

MAKES 4 SERVINGS

4 cloves garlic, sliced

1 tbsp finely chopped cilantro root (see page 157)

3 to 4 Thai bird chiles, minced

1 tsp cracked black peppercorns

2 tbsp canola or peanut oil

1 lb squid, body and tentacles cut into bite-size pieces

1 cup red bell pepper julienne

1 cup chicken broth

½ cup sliced scallions, cut on the diagonal into ½ inch pieces

2 tbsp oyster sauce

2 tbsp fish sauce

1 tbsp sugar

1 cup Thai basil leaves, whole

Steamed jasmine rice, optional (see page 160)

1. Pound the garlic, cilantro root, chiles, and peppercorns together in a mortar and pestle to make a paste or grind the ingredients together with a food processor.

2. Heat the oil in a wok over high heat until nearly smoking. Add the garlic-chile paste and stir-fry until aromatic, about 1 minute.

3. Add the squid pieces to the wok and stir-fry until the squid just starts to change color and is evenly coated with the garlic-chile paste, about 3 minutes. Add the bell pepper and stir-fry until very hot, about 2 minutes.

4. Add the chicken broth, scallions, oyster sauce, fish sauce, and sugar. Continue to cook over medium heat until the squid is cooked through but still tender, about 3 minutes.

5. Add the basil and toss well. Serve in heated shallow plates with steamed jasmine rice, if desired.

cockles with chorizo

in a Garlic, Wine, and Parsley Sauce

*I*F YOU cannot locate cockles for this dish, try it with littleneck clams or mussels. The combination of bold flavors in this dish makes a memorable, quick-to-cook dinner.

MAKES 6 SERVINGS

3 tbsp olive oil

½ cup sliced Spanish-style chorizo

½ cup minced onion, finely chopped

3 garlic cloves, sliced thin

½ cup dry white wine

½ cup clam broth or water

1 bay leaf

1 tbsp lemon juice

3 tbsp minced parsley

4 dozen cockles or manila clams, cleaned (see note, page 119)

1. Heat the oil in a skillet over medium heat until it shimmers. Add the chorizo, onion, and garlic and sauté, stirring frequently, until the onion is softened, about 10 minutes.

2. Add the wine and simmer rapidly until most of the wine has cooked away, about 5 minutes. Reduce the heat to medium-high and add the clam broth or water, bay leaf, lemon juice, and 2 tablespoons parsley. Add the cockles and cook over high heat, shaking the pan constantly, for 1 to 2 minutes. Cover the pan and cook until the cockles open, about 10 minutes. Discard any that remain closed.

3. Serve the cockles in heated pasta bowls or soup plates. Spoon the sauce over the cockles, sprinkle with the remaining parsley, and serve immediately.

mussels with olives

Mejillones al Estilo de Laredo

*i*N THIS Spanish-inspired recipe for mussels, a sauce enriched with olives and wine is a perfect counterpoint to the sweet and briny mussels. Serve this dish with lots of crusty bread for soaking up the sauce.

MAKES 4 SERVINGS

6 dozen mussels

2 tbsp olive oil

1 small yellow onion, sliced thin

2 anchovy fillets, chopped

⅛ tsp red pepper flakes

1 tbsp minced shallot

1 tsp minced garlic

1½ cups diced plum tomatoes

¼ cup dry white wine

1 bay leaf

Salt as needed

Freshly ground black pepper as needed

¼ cup chopped or sliced black olives, pitted and chopped

2 tbsp chopped flat-leaf parsley for garnish

1. Scrub the mussels under running cold water with a stiff-bristled brush and remove their beards (see page 119). Set aside.

2. Heat the oil in a casserole or Dutch oven over high heat until it shimmers. Add the onion and sauté, stirring occasionally, until translucent, about 6 minutes. Add the anchovy fillets and red pepper flakes and stir until the anchovies break apart and "dissolve." Add the shallot and garlic and sauté, stirring constantly, until aromatic, about 30 seconds. Add the tomatoes, wine, bay leaf, and a pinch of salt and pepper. Bring to a boil over medium-high heat.

3. Add the mussels to the casserole, cover tightly, and steam until the mussels open, about 12 minutes. Discard any mussels that do not open. Scoop the mussels into a large heated bowl or individual bowls. Stir the olives into the sauce remaining in the casserole and season to taste with salt and pepper. Spoon the sauce over the mussels, garnish with parsley, and serve at once.

prosciutto-wrapped hake

with Herb-Roasted Vegetables and Lentils

HAKE, ALSO commonly referred to as whiting, is a white-fleshed fish which is part of the cod family. If you can't find it at your local fish market, you might also try cod, haddock, halibut, or grouper prepared in this manner.

MAKES 4 SERVINGS

1 cup diced carrot

1 cup diced parsnip

1 cup diced Hubbard squash or pumpkin

½ cup diced tomato

½ cup diced yellow onion

2 tsp minced garlic

1 tbsp minced fresh basil

½ tsp minced fresh oregano

3 tbsp olive oil

Salt, as needed

Freshly ground pepper, as needed

4 hake fillets (about 6 oz each)

Juice of ½ lemon

4 slices prosciutto

2 cups cooked green or brown lentils

½ cup chicken broth, or as needed

Shaved fennel and fennel tops for garnish

Lamb's lettuce (mâche) for garnish

1. Preheat the oven to 375°F. Toss together the carrot, parsnip, squash or pumpkin, tomato, onion, garlic, basil, oregano, and 2 tablespoons olive oil in a roasting pan or baking dish. Season with salt and pepper. Place in the oven and roast, stirring occasionally, until the vegetables are tender and browned, about 30 minutes.

2. Season the fish with salt and pepper and squeeze half the lemon half over it. Wrap a piece of prosciutto around each fillet and use a toothpick or skewer to secure it if needed.

3. Heat the remaining oil in a large sauté pan over medium-high heat until it shimmers. Add the fillets and sear on the first side just until the fish is lightly colored and the prosciutto is crisp, about 3 minutes. Carefully turn and continue cooking until the other side is lightly colored, about 4 minutes. Transfer from the pan with a slotted spoon, letting any juices from the fish drain back into the pan. Keep hot.

4. Remove the vegetables from the oven and add them to the sauté pan. Add the lentils and a small amount of broth, if necessary, to keep the mixture moist but not soupy. Reduce the heat to medium and sauté, stirring frequently, until the lentils and vegetables are very hot and flavorful, about 5 minutes. Season to taste with salt, pepper, and additional lemon juice.

5. Serve the hake with the vegetables and lentils on heated plates. Garnish with shaved fennel and lamb's lettuce.

sautéed shrimp with ancho chiles and garlic

aNCHO CHILES give a deep flavor to this dish. If you enjoy a bit more heat, add a teaspoon or two of chopped chipotle chiles and bit of the adobo sauce they are packed in along with the ancho chiles in this recipe.

MAKES 4 SERVINGS

¾ cup olive oil

2 garlic cloves, peeled and thinly sliced

1¾ lb rock shrimp, peeled and deveined

Salt as needed

Freshly ground black pepper as needed

3 fresh ancho chiles, seeded and cut into matchsticks

1 cup fish or clam broth

3 tbsp lime juice

¼ cup chopped flat-leaf parsley

Steamed white rice, optional (see page 160)

1. Heat the olive oil in a large skillet over medium-low heat until it shimmers. Sauté the garlic slices, stirring frequently, until tender but not brown, about 5 minutes. Transfer with a slotted spoon to paper towels and reserve.

2. Increase the heat to high. In a bowl, quickly toss the shrimp with the salt and pepper. When oil is nearly smoking, add the shrimp. Sauté, stirring as necessary, until the shrimp are brightly colored but not cooked through, about 3 minutes. Transfer the shrimp to a platter using a slotted spoon, leaving as much liquid as possible in the pan.

3. Reduce heat to medium. Add the reserved garlic slices and the ancho chiles. Sauté, stirring frequently, until the oil begins to turn orange from the chiles, about 1 minute. Stir in the fish or clam both, along with the shrimp and any juice that has collected on the platter. Add the lime juice and parsley, bring to a boil, and immediately remove the pan from the heat.

4. Serve immediately in heated soup plates with steamed white rice, if desired.

shrimp with tomatoes, oregano, and feta cheese

To MAKE this dish even more interesting, you may want to quickly broil it once you've added the cheese. Feta cheese doesn't melt the way cheddar or mozzarella does. It simply softens and begins to brown around the edges.

MAKES 4 SERVINGS

1½ lb large shrimp (16/20 count), shelled and deveined

Salt as needed

Freshly ground black pepper as needed

2 tbsp olive oil

1 cup chopped yellow onion

2 tsp minced garlic

¼ tsp ground cayenne

2 tbsp chopped oregano

1 cup Tomato Sauce (page 165)

1 tsp sugar

1 cup crumbled feta cheese

¼ cup chopped flat-leaf parsley

4 slices crusty bread

1. Season the shrimp with salt and pepper. Heat the oil in a large sauté pan over high heat until it shimmers. Add the shrimp and sauté, turning as necessary, until the shrimp are a bright pink, 2 to 3 minutes. Transfer the shrimp to a plate and keep warm.

2. Add the onion, garlic, cayenne, and oregano to the pan and sauté, stirring constantly, until aromatic, about 1 minute. Add the tomato sauce, reduce the heat to low, and bring to a simmer. Season the sauce to taste with sugar, salt, and pepper. Return the shrimp to the sauce and simmer very slowly until the shrimp is completely cooked, about 5 minutes.

3. Transfer the shrimp to a serving dish (or individual gratin dishes). Top the shrimp with the sauce and sprinkle the cheese evenly over the top. Serve very hot, topped with the chopped parsley. Serve with crusty bread.

jungle curry

GALANGAL IS an essential ingredient in this dish. You can often find this rhizome in some specialty markets, but if you can't find a source for fresh galangal, fresh ginger root would be a better replacement than either powdered or dried galangal root in this recipe. To learn more about some of the ingredients featured in this dish, see the note below.

MAKES 4 SERVINGS

2 tbsp peanut oil

2 tbsp minced garlic

¼ cup Jungle Curry Paste (recipe follows)

1 lb boneless pork shoulder, cubed

2 cups chicken broth

1 lb Thai eggplant, quartered

½ lb long beans, cut into 1-inch lengths

¼ cup thinly sliced galangal root

4 wild lime leaves, chopped

¼ cup fish sauce

1 cup Thai basil leaves

Salt as needed

Sticky rice, optional (see page 160)

1. Heat a wok over high heat. Add the oil and heat until it is nearly smoking. Add the garlic and curry paste and fry until aromatic, about 2 minutes.

2. Add the cubed pork and stir-fry until browned on all sides, about 6 minutes.

3. Add the broth, bring to a simmer, and continue to cook over medium heat until the pork is tender and cooked through, another 10 minutes.

4. Add the eggplant, beans, galangal, lime leaves, and fish sauce. Continue to cook until the eggplant is tender, about 10 minutes.

5. Remove from the heat and stir in basil leaves. Season to taste with salt. Serve with sticky rice, if desired.

Jungle Curry Paste

MAKES ¼ CUP

6 shallots, chopped

1 tbsp chopped garlic

1 tsp salt

2 tbsp minced galangal

1½ tbsp minced lemongrass

8 small dried red chiles, crushed

2 wild lime leaves

2 tsp Thai shrimp paste

Place shallots, garlic, and salt into a mortar, a spice grinder, or a small food processor and grind to a paste. Continue to add the remaining ingredients one at a time, grinding into a smooth paste. The curry paste is ready to use now or it can be stored in a covered jar in the refrigerator for up to 2 days.

THAI INGREDIENTS

Thai cuisine calls for a number of ingredients that once were difficult to find unless you lived near a thriving Asian community.

Galangal is one such ingredient. It looks and tastes a little like fresh ginger, but adds a unique flavor you cannot get from ginger alone.

Thai basil, sometimes known as anise basil or holy basil, has deep green leaves that are smaller and more pointed than Western basil leaves. They grow on purplish stems topped with pretty, reddish-purple flower buds. You can substitute other basils for Thai basil if necessary.

mushroom-cauliflower curry

tHAI BIRD chiles give this dish some heat. You can use more than two, as we've suggested here, as long as you know your guests' tolerance level for hot chiles.

MAKES 6 SERVINGS

⅓ cup olive or canola oil

1½ cups chopped onion

2 tbsp chopped ginger root

2 tbsp chopped garlic

2 tsp cumin seeds

2 red bell peppers, cut into medium dice

1 green bell pepper, sweet, cut into medium dice

2 Thai bird chiles, chopped

4 tsp Indian or Korean chili powder

2 tsp ground turmeric

2 tsp ground coriander

1 cup water

2 cups chopped plum tomato

1 cup tomato puree

1 tbsp tomato paste

1 tbsp garam masala

4 cups cauliflower florets (thawed if frozen)

4 cups white mushrooms, sliced or quartered if desired

Salt as needed

Lemon juice as needed

Freshly ground black pepper as needed

1 cup chopped cilantro

1. Heat the oil in a sauté pan over medium high heat until it shimmers. Add the onion and sauté, stirring frequently, until light golden brown, 10 to 12 minutes.

2. Add the ginger root, garlic, and cumin seeds. Sauté over low heat until aromatic, about 2 minutes. Add the red and green peppers and the Thai bird chiles. Sauté, stirring frequently, until the peppers are limp, another 2 minutes.

3. In a small bowl, mix the chili powder, turmeric, and coriander with the water. Pour this mixture into the sauté pan and simmer over high heat until all of the moisture has evaporated, 6 to 7 minutes.

4. Add the chopped tomato, tomato puree, tomato paste, and garam masala. Sauté, stirring constantly, until the mixture is thickened and has a sweet aroma, about 5 minutes.

5. When the mixture is cooked and oil begins to collect at the sides of the pan, add the cauliflower florets and mushrooms. Stir well and season to taste with salt. Bring the curry to a boil and then reduce the heat to low. Cover the pan and simmer, stirring occasionally, until the cauliflower is tender and the curry is very flavorful, about 12 minutes.

6. Season the curry with lemon juice, salt, and pepper. Sprinkle with the cilantro and serve in heated soup plates.

Wild lime leaves add sharpness to dishes. Lemon or lime zest can be substituted if you can't locate fresh wild lime leaves.

Cilantro is stocked in most grocery stores. Select bunches of cilantro that still have the roots attached, if you can find them. Many Southeast

Asian dishes call for the root. Once you've thoroughly rinsed the root, chop it very fine with a chef's knife.

Fish sauce, curry pastes, and coconut milk are ubiquitous in curries and stir-fries. Taste several varieties to find the one you like best.

bibimbap

CONTRASTING TEMPERATURES and textures make this dish an adventure. Freshly fried eggs and marinated strips of steak are served on a bed of cool, crisp vegetables, all set atop a mound of hot steamed rice.

MAKES 4 SERVINGS

BEEF MARINADE

¼ cup Korean soy sauce

2 tsp sugar

¼ cup minced scallions

1 tbsp minced garlic

2 tsp minced ginger root

2 tsp ground toasted sesame seeds

Few drops dark sesame oil, as needed

Freshly ground black pepper, as needed

1 lb beef skirt steak, cut into strips

¼ cup peanut or canola oil, as needed

2 cups steamed medium-grained rice (see page 160)

2 cups iceberg lettuce chiffonade

1 cup julienned or grated red radish

1 cup julienned or grated daikon

1 cup julienned or grated carrot

1 cup julienned or grated seedless cucumber

4 shiso leaves, cut into fine shreds

4 large eggs

2 tbsp Korean red pepper paste (gochujang), or as needed

1. Combine the soy sauce and sugar in a bowl. Add the scallions, garlic, ginger, and sesame seeds. Add the sesame oil and pepper to taste. Add the skirt steak and toss until evenly coated. Cover, refrigerate, and let the steak marinate for at least 1 and up to 8 hours.

2. Heat 2 tablespoons oil in a wok over high heat until it is nearly smoking. Add the beef strips to the hot oil and stir-fry until the beef is cooked, about 4 minutes. Transfer to a bowl and keep warm.

3. Divide the rice evenly among 4 bowls. Top the rice with the lettuce. Toss together the red radish, daikon, carrot, cucumber, and shiso leaves. Divide the vegetables evenly among the bowls. Top the vegetables with the skirt steak and season each serving with a few drops of dark sesame oil.

4. Wipe out the wok and return it to the burner. Add 1 tablespoon oil to the wok and heat over medium heat until the oil ripples. Add the eggs to the hot oil one at a time and fry, basting the top with a little oil, until the whites are set and the yolk is hot, 2 to 3 minutes. Top each serving with a fried egg and serve at once, accompanied by the Korean red pepper paste.

SHISO LEAVES

Shiso leaves, sometimes known as perillo, come from an herb related to both basil and mint. In fact, it is similar in flavor to those herbs, although most would agree that shiso leaves have a more complex flavor than either herb.

Green shiso leaves are typically used in salads, stir-fries, or in tempura. Red shiso leaves are used to flavor and color Japan's famous pickled plums, umeboshi. If you can't find shiso leaves, you can use either basil or mint, or both.

fried rice with chinese sausage

gOOD FRIED rice calls for cold, cooked rice. Steam the rice according to the instructions below, then chill it overnight in the refrigerator. Before you use it to make fried rice, break up the clumps of rice into individual grains. Wet your hands with cool water and rub the rice until it separates.

MAKES 6 SERVINGS

2 tbsp peanut or light sesame oil

½ lb Chinese sausage, cut into medium dice

1½ cups minced onion

⅔ cup medium-dice carrot

½ cup sliced shiitake mushroom caps

¾ cup red or green bell pepper, cut into strips

2 cups shredded Napa cabbage

6 cups steamed long-grain rice, cold (see note below)

Salt as needed

Freshly ground black pepper as needed

1½ cups snow peas, sliced on the diagonal

3 large eggs, lightly beaten

2 tbsp mushroom soy sauce

1. Heat the oil in wok over medium heat until it shimmers. Add the diced sausage and stir-fry until the fat is released and the sausage is very hot, about 3 minutes. Add the onion and continue to stir-fry until golden, 4 to 5 minutes.

2. Add the carrot and stir-fry until hot, about 2 minutes. Add the mushrooms and stir-fry until they begin to release a little moisture, about 2 minutes. Add the peppers and stir-fry until they are limp, about 2 minutes. Add the cabbage and stir-fry until the cabbage is very hot, about 2 minutes.

3. Add the rice and stir-fry until rice is hot and begins to brown. Season to taste with salt and pepper. When the rice begins to turn golden in spots, add the snow peas and stir-fry until they are bright green, about 3 minutes.

4. Pour the beaten eggs into the wok around the edge of the rice. Leave the eggs undisturbed until they begin to turn opaque, then fold them into the rice and cook until the eggs are set and the dish is very hot, about 3 minutes. Season to taste with mushroom soy sauce, salt, and pepper. Serve at once on a heated platter or plates.

STEAMED RICE

Steamed rice is a perfect backdrop to many of the dishes featured in this book. Perfectly steamed rice should be hot and fragrant. The type of rice you choose will have an effect on the cooked grain's texture. Jasmine or basmati rice has long kernels that are dry and have a tendency to separate. Sticky rice, as well as short- and medium-grain varieties, is moister with a greater tendency to hold together. Saffron rice has a rich golden hue.

Measure the rice, planning on about 1 cup dried rice for 6 people. Combine the rice and 2 cups cold water in a sauce pan. Add about 1 teaspoon salt (more or less to your taste) and bring the water to a boil over high heat. (For saffron rice, add 4 or 5 crushed saffron threads.) Immediately turn the heat to low, cover the pan tightly, and cook until the rice is tender. Check the rice from time to time as it steams; you may need to add a bit more water if the pot is dry but the rice is still crunchy. White rice usually take about 15 minutes. Brown rice can take anywhere from 35 to 45 minutes.

pork cutlets with mushrooms and spinach

Escalope de Porc Forestière

FORESTIÈRE, OR "of the forest," refers to the use of wild mushrooms in a dish. Nowadays, many of the wild mushrooms sold in supermarkets are in fact cultivated, and as a result are available year-round, instead of only in their natural season. Wavy-capped, apricot-colored chanterelle mushrooms are an exception, since they are still usually foraged rather than cultivated; look for them at farmers' markets in the autumn and spring.

MAKES 4 SERVINGS

8 boneless pork cutlets (from the loin, about 3 oz each)

Salt, as needed

Freshly ground black pepper, as needed

16 thin slices sopressata

All-purpose flour for dredging

½ cup canola oil, or as needed

1 small shallot, minced

6 cups lightly packed spinach leaves, rinsed and dried

2 tbsp unsalted butter

1 cup sliced assorted mushrooms

1 tsp fresh thyme leaves

¼ cup dry white wine

¼ cup beef or chicken broth

1. Season the pork with salt and pepper. Top each cutlet with two slices of sopressata. Dredge in the flour. Pour enough oil into a large sauté pan to come to a depth of ¼ inch and heat over high heat until the oil shimmers. Add the pork and pan-fry on the first side until deep golden brown, 3 to 4 minutes. Turn the pork and continue cooking on the second side until the pork is cooked through and the exterior is golden brown, 3 to 4 minutes more. Transfer to a warmed platter and cover to keep warm.

2. Pour off all but 2 tablespoons oil and return the pan to medium heat. Add the shallot and sauté, stirring constantly, until limp, about 1 minute. Increase the heat to high, add the spinach by handfuls and sauté until the spinach is limp and deep green, about 5 minutes. Transfer to a plate and keep warm.

3. Return the pan to high heat and heat 1 tablespoon of the butter until it stops foaming. Add the mushrooms and thyme, and sauté until the mushrooms are lightly browned, about 2 minutes.

4. Add the wine and stir to deglaze the pan, scraping up any browned bits from the bottom of the pan. Add the broth and any juices released by the pork. Simmer over high heat until the liquid has reduced by about half, 6 to 7 minutes. Swirl in the remaining butter to thicken the sauce slightly. Serve the pork cutlets and spinach at once on heated plates with the mushrooms.

spicy pork with green chiles

Qing Jao Rouding

SWEET AND sour flavors combine with spicy Thai bird chiles in this stir-fry. A quickly applied coating of cornstarch and egg white gives the pork an appealing texture when it is stir-fried.

MAKES 6 SERVINGS

2 lb boneless pork loin

1 large egg

½ cup cornstarch

½ cup light rice vinegar

¼ cup light soy sauce

¼ cup chicken broth

3 tbsp sake (rice wine)

⅓ cup sugar

2 tsp sesame oil

¼ cup canola oil

1 tsp minced ginger root

1 tsp minced garlic

2 tbsp thinly sliced scallion

2 tbsp minced Thai bird chile (with seeds)

1 cup large-dice red bell pepper

1 cup large-dice green frying pepper

1 cup thinly sliced white mushroom caps

Pan-roasted cashews (page 44) for garnish, optional

1. Cut the pork into ½-inch dice. Whisk together the egg and ¼ cup of cornstarch; toss the pork with this mixture to coat evenly. Cover and refrigerate for at least 1 and up to 3 hours.

2. Combine the rice vinegar, soy sauce, chicken broth, sake, sugar, and sesame oil. Stir in the remaining cornstarch. Set the mixture aside.

3. Heat a wok over high heat, add the oil, and heat until nearly smoking. Add the ginger, garlic, scallion, and Thai bird chile. Stir-fry until aromatic, about 1 minute.

4. Add the pork and stir-fry until the pork is half cooked and lightly colored on all sides, about 2 minutes. Add the bell and frying peppers and the mushrooms and stir-fry until they are tender and the pork is cooked through, 5 to 6 minutes.

5. Stir the vinegar-soy sauce mixture to blend in the cornstarch if it has settled at the bottom. Pour this mixture into the wok while stirring constantly. Continue to stir-fry over high heat until the mixture is thickened and the ingredients are evenly coated.

6. Garnish with cashews, if desired, and serve immediately on heated plates.

sautéed chicken

with Moroccan Hot and Sweet Tomato Sauce

gINGER AND cinnamon give the tomato sauce its heat, while dark honey gives it a touch of sweetness. If you can't find the dark honey called for in the recipe, try using either Grade B maple syrup or molasses.

MAKES 4 SERVINGS

½ cup chopped onion

2 tsp minced garlic

4 boneless skinless chicken breast pieces (about 6 ounces each)

Salt as needed

Freshly ground black pepper as needed

2 tbsp olive oil, plus as needed

2 tbsp butter

¾ tsp ground cinnamon

¼ tsp ground ginger

Pinch cayenne pepper or as needed

1 cup Tomato Sauce (recipe follows)

1 tbsp dark honey

1 tbsp sesame seeds, toasted

2 tbsp chopped cilantro leaves

1. Puree the onion and garlic in a food processor until a coarse paste forms. Set aside.

2. Blot the chicken dry and season with salt and pepper. Heat the olive oil in a casserole or Dutch oven over medium-high heat until it shimmers. Add the chicken pieces (do not overcrowd the pan; work in batches until all chicken is prepared and add more oil as needed) and sauté on the first side until about 2 to 3 minutes. Turn the chicken and sauté on the second side for another 3 minutes. Lower the heat if necessary to avoid scorching the chicken. Transfer to plate and keep warm.

3. Heat the butter in the pan over medium heat. Add the onion and garlic puree and cook, stirring frequently, until the onion is tender and has a sweet smell, about 10 minutes. Stir in the cinnamon, ginger, and cayenne and cook for another 2 to 3 minutes. Add the tomato sauce and honey to the pan and simmer for another 5 minutes. Season to taste with salt and pepper.

4. Return the chicken to the pan. Spoon the sauce over the chicken pieces, cover, and cook over low heat until the chicken is fully cooked, about 20 minutes. Sprinkle the sesame seeds and cilantro over the chicken before serving.

Tomato Sauce

MAKES 2 CUPS SAUCE

2 cups whole plum tomatoes, peeled and seeded

1 cup tomato puree

2 tbsp butter, sliced and chilled

Salt as needed

Freshly ground black pepper as needed

Puree the whole tomatoes in a food processor until a coarse paste forms. Transfer the tomatoes to a saucepan and bring to a simmer over low heat. Add the tomato puree and continue to simmer for another 10 minutes. Scatter the sliced butter over the tomato sauce and swirl the pan until the butter is incorporated. Season to taste with salt and pepper.

light fare

MANY OF THE meals we associate with one dish cooking are big, bountiful recipes perfect for the main meal of the day. When the weather is sultry or the farmer's market is bursting at the seams with fresh produce, your appetite may call out for meals that are lighter. Salads, sandwiches, and pizzas fill that need.

The list of recipes in this chapter reads like a culinary journey around the world, from the famous sub sandwiches served on the streets of Saigon to the po'boys of New Orleans. We've featured them as the focus of the meal. You may be inclined to serve some of these offerings along with a bowl of soup or chili.

Rounding out a One Dish Meal with a Simple Green Salad

Much as we love the idea of a one dish salad or sandwich, we also know that it's important to keep the meal lively. To that end, we suggest including a simple green salad for many of the dishes throughout this book, including the sandwiches and pizzas here. Green salads are often an element in a main course salad, either tossed into the salad or served as a bed for other ingredients.

Select the freshest, most appealing greens you can find. Opt for salad mixes or blends, if you wish, or visit your favorite salad bar. When you are ready to make the salad, thoroughly rinse and dry the greens (even if the bag says triple-washed).

Next, put the ingredients for your dressing into a large bowl. For every person, add 1 tablespoon of good oil and 1 teaspoon of good vinegar, a pinch of salt, some fresh pepper, and a sprinkling of minced fresh herbs. Whisk these ingredients together and dunk a lettuce leaf into the dressing to taste it. Make any adjustments you like now and then tumble the greens into the bowl. Turn the greens in the dressing until everything is evenly coated and serve.

Rounding out a One Dish Meal with a Bountiful Spread

Some salads, like our Turkish-inspired Roasted Eggplant Salad, may motivate you to go to your favorite market to select a wide variety of side items like pita bread, olives, pickles, raw and marinated vegetables, olive oil, or cheeses. Salads like the Greek Bread Salad or an Italian inspired salad of farro (whole kernel wheat) make a platter of sliced or smoked meats, cheeses, and breads into a feast.

vietnamese salad rolls

DESPITE ITS common name of Vietnamese mint (or hot mint), *rau ram* is not related to the mint family, but is actually a member of the buckwheat family. Rau ram has long, smooth green leaves on a purple tinged stem. Its aroma is described as a combination of lemon and coriander-cilantro aroma and it has a bitter, peppery flavor. If you cannot locate *rau ram,* you can substitute ordinary mint.

MAKES 8 SERVINGS

DIPPING SAUCE

¼ cup fish sauce

¼ cup sugar, plus 2 tbsp for rice wrappers

¼ cup water

3 tbsp rice vinegar

4 tsp chili sauce

2 tsp minced garlic

Juice of 1 lime

4 oz rice noodles

2 cups carrot julienne

Salt as needed

½ bunch green-leaf lettuce, cut into thin strips

¼ bunch mint leaves (or rau ram), torn in thin strips

4 cups warm water

8 rice paper rounds, 12-inch diameter

16 small cooked shrimp (30/35 count), peeled, deveined, and halved lengthwise

¼ bunch cilantro leaves

1. Combine the fish sauce, ¼ cup sugar, ¼ cup water, vinegar, chili sauce, garlic, and lime juice to make a dipping sauce. Mix well and chill if made ahead of time. The sauce may be held for up to 24 hours.

2. Bring a large pot of salted water to a boil. Add the rice noodles, stir once or twice, and cook until tender, about 3 minutes. Drain the noodles and then rinse with cool water until they are chilled. Drain well and set aside.

3. Marinate the carrot with 2 teaspoons salt for 10 minutes. Rinse in cool water to remove the salt and squeeze out the juice from the carrots. Set aside.

4. Combine rice noodles, marinated carrots, lettuce, and mint to make the noodle filling. Set aside.

5. Combine 4 cups warm water with 2 tablespoons sugar in a bowl. Place the rice papers, one at a time, in the water until they soften, about 10 seconds. Remove the rice paper, blot on paper toweling, and transfer to a work surface. Spoon ½ cup of the noodle filling in the center of each rice paper. Roll the rice paper around the filling halfway. Put two pieces shrimp and two or three cilantro leaves on the inside of the unrolled part of the wrapper and finish rolling.

6. Cut each roll in half and serve on chilled platters or plates with the dipping sauce.

CLOCKWISE FROM UPPER LEFT *To prepare the vegetables for the rolls, julienne them into matchsticks about two inches long and ⅛-inch thick. Rice paper is made pliable and easy to work with when it is rehydrated in cold water just before use. When rolling the fillings up inside the rice paper, begin at the bottom of the rice paper and roll away from you. As you pass the middle, bring both sides of the paper in to the center, then keep them tucked in as you complete the roll. The finished rolls are best served cold with a hot & spicy dipping sauce.*

greek bread salad

i N COMMUNITIES where bread-baking is a once-a-week tradition, recipes that make use of dried bread are common. This dish, similar to the famous Italian bread salad known as panzanella, is deceptively filling. Paximadi is the name of dried bread, or rusks, made from barley bread. Look for it in shops that specialize in Greek or Turkish foods.

MAKES 6 SERVINGS

2½ cups extra virgin olive oil

1½ cups pitted kalamata olives

¾ cup capers, drained

6 pepperoncini, seeded and sliced into thin strips

6 garlic cloves, thinly sliced

6 beefsteak tomatoes, peeled, seeded, and chopped

Zest and juice of 3 lemons

Salt as needed

6 paximadi (dry barley rusks)

1 cup crumbled feta cheese

2 tbsp dried Greek oregano

1 bunch flat leaf parsley, coarsely chopped

1. Combine the olive oil, olives, capers, pepperoncini, and garlic in a large bowl. Cover and let marinate at room temperature for 4 to 6 hours.

2. Mix together the chopped tomatoes, lemon juice and zest, and salt in a bowl. Set aside.

3. To assemble the salad: Dip the paximadi in water and gently shake off any excess liquid. Place one rusk in the center of each plate. Spoon a generous ¼ cup of the tomato mixture over the rusks and let them absorb the juices for about 10 minutes before serving. Spoon a few tablespoons of olive mixture over the tomatoes and top with an equal amount of crumbled feta. Sprinkle a large pinch of oregano over the cheese. Garnish each plate with a generous amount of chopped parsley.

farro salad

Insalata di Farro

FARRO IS an ancestor to the wheat grown today. It was the primary ingredient in *puls*, the polenta eaten for centuries by the Roman poor before corn was introduced from the New World. Farro has a pleasant, chewy texture and it absorbs other flavors beautifully. The salad also is delicious made with barley instead of farro.

MAKES 4 SERVINGS

3 cups water

Salt as needed

1 cup farro, soaked in cold water for 1 hour

¼ cup lemon juice

6 or 7 mint sprigs

¼ cup red wine vinegar

¼ cup chopped fresh mint

Pinch of sugar, or as needed

1¼ cups extra-virgin olive oil

Freshly ground black pepper as needed

2 beefsteak tomatoes, seeded and chopped

½ cup diced seeded cucumber

½ cup diced celery or fennel

½ cup diced red or yellow bell pepper

⅓ cup diced red onion

¼ cup chopped fresh basil or mint

¼ cup chopped flat leaf parsley

1. Bring 3 cups of lightly salted water to a boil over high heat in a saucepan. Add the farro and stir once or twice to separate the grains. Reduce the heat to medium and simmer, covered, until the farro doubles in volume and is tender to the bite, 25 to 30 minutes. Drain the farro, if necessary, transfer it to a salad bowl, and cool to room temperature. Set aside.

2. To make the dressing: Combine the lemon juice and mint sprigs in a small pan and bring to a boil over high heat. Immediately remove the pan from the heat, cover, and let the mint infuse the lemon juice until flavorful, about 10 minutes. Remove and discard the mint sprigs. Whisk in the vinegar, mint, and a pinch of sugar. Add the oil while whisking until the dressing is blended and lightly thickened. Season to taste with salt and pepper.

3. Add the tomatoes, cucumber, celery or fennel, bell pepper, red onion, basil or mint, and parsley to the farro. Pour the dressing over the salad ingredients and fold the salad together until it is evenly dressed. Serve on chilled plates.

roasted eggplant salad

tHIS EGGPLANT salad makes a great dip or even a filling for a sandwich, but to make it the center of a meal, serve it with plenty of pita bread, olives, feta cheese, and nuts.

3 lb eggplant (1 large or 2 medium)

2 to 3 lemons

¼ cup extra-virgin olive oil, plus as needed

4 tbsp finely chopped flat leaf parsley

4 garlic cloves, minced

2 tsp ground cumin

Salt as needed

Freshly ground black pepper as needed

½ cup crumbled feta cheese

1 cup thinly sliced cucumber

4 plum tomatoes, sliced thin

¼ cup cured olives

1 green pepper, roasted, seeded, and cut into strips

½ cup coarsely chopped toasted walnuts

4 pita breads, warmed

1. For a smoky taste, grill eggplants under the broiler, turning often, or cook them slowly on a stovetop cast iron griddle. You also can bake them at 400 degrees F until the eggplants are soft throughout. Drain in a colander.

2. Halve the lemons and squeeze the juice. Set the juice aside and put the peels into a small bowl of cold water. When the eggplants are cool enough to handle, strip away the skin and scoop out and discard any large seed pockets. Place remaining eggplant pulp in the lemon water. After a few minutes, drain the eggplant pulp and squeeze dry.

3. Mash the eggplant in bowl and blend in the olive oil, lemon juice, chopped parsley, garlic, and cumin. Season to taste with additional olive oil, lemon juice, salt, and pepper.

4. Chill well before serving on chilled plates garnished with feta cheese, slices of cucumber, tomato, olives, green pepper, and walnuts. Accompany the salad with warm pita bread.

warm vegetables and tofu on cool noodles

THE CONTRAST of temperatures in this dish is intriguing. The rice noodles are sold in sticks and may be labeled as *mee fun*.

MAKES 4 SERVINGS

SOY DIPPING SAUCE

¼ cup lime juice

¼ cup soy sauce

3 tbsp rice wine vinegar

3 tbsp mirin

2 tsp tamari sauce

2 tbsp chopped cilantro

8 dried shiitake mushrooms

1 block firm tofu, pressed and drained (page 142)

¾ lb dried rice vermicelli

2 cups bean sprouts

2 cucumbers, seeded and shredded

4 cups shredded romaine lettuce

¾ cup coarsely chopped mint leaves

2 tbsp peanut or canola oil

1 medium onion, sliced ¼-inch thick

2 cups carrot julienne

2 cups broccoli florets, blanched

2 cups Napa cabbage, sliced in ½-inch-thick slices

1 cup red bell pepper strips

2 tbsp soy sauce

1 tsp sugar, or as needed

¼ cup roughly chopped pan-roasted peanuts

¾ cup thinly sliced scallions

1. Stir together the ingredients for the dipping sauce in a small bowl and set aside.

2. Rehydrate the shiitake mushrooms in cool water until softened (see page 91). Cut off the entire stem and discard. Cut the caps into ¼-inch wide strips and set aside. Cut the tofu into strips of about the same size and set aside.

3. Soak the vermicelli in warm water for 20 minutes, drain, and cook in boiling water until tender, 2 to 3 minutes. Drain and rinse under cold running water. Drain well and transfer to a salad bowl.

4. Gently toss the cooked vermicelli with the bean sprouts, cucumbers, romaine lettuce, and mint until the ingredients are evenly distributed.

5. Heat the oil in a wok over high heat until it is nearly smoking. Add the onion and mushrooms and stir-fry until aromatic, about 2 minutes. Add the carrot, broccoli, cabbage, red bell pepper, and tofu and stir-fry for an additional 2 to 3 minutes. Add the soy sauce and continue to stir-fry until all of the ingredients are coated and very hot, about 2 minutes. Remove from the heat and season to taste with sugar.

6. Make a bed of the noodle-bean sprout mixture on a chilled platter or plates. Top with the stir-fried vegetables. Garnish with roasted peanuts and scallions. Serve with the dipping sauce.

lobster and roasted red pepper salad

RICH-TASTING AND gorgeous-looking, this is an elegant salad that can be assembled in minutes. Serve it as a first course or accompanied with crusty bread for a light dinner. You can cook the lobster up to 2 days ahead of serving. Remove the meat and refrigerate. Keep chilled until it is time to assemble the salad. You can also look for cooked lobster meat at the market.

MAKES 8 SERVINGS

1 tbsp lemon juice

1 tbsp thyme leaves

2 tbsp extra-virgin olive oil

Salt as needed

Freshly ground black pepper as needed

8 cups mixed salad greens, cleaned and dried

4 roasted red bell peppers, peeled, seeded, and cut into strips

1 cup corn kernels, fresh or frozen

1 jalapeño pepper, seeded and sliced into thin rings

1 pint cherry tomatoes

4 steamed lobsters, 1½ lb each, meat removed from shell (see note at right)

1. Whisk together the lemon juice, thyme, and oil in a large salad bowl. Season with salt and pepper to taste.

2. Add the greens and gently toss to coat. Using tongs, lift the greens and let the dressing drain back into the bowl. Transfer to chilled plates or a platter.

3. Add the peppers, corn, and jalapeño to the dressing remaining in the bowl and toss to coat thoroughly.

4. Arrange the vegetables and tomatoes on top of greens. Lean one of the claws against the salad and fan half of a lobster tail next to the claw.

WORKING WITH LOBSTER

To steam live lobsters, put about 1 inch of water and a steamer insert in a large pot with a lid, cover, and bring to a boil over high heat. Add the lobsters, replace the cover, and steam until the shells are bright red/pink and the flesh is opaque and cooked through, 10 to 12 minutes. Remove the lobsters and let them cool until they can be handled. Use kitchen shears or a heavy duty knife to cut through the lobster shell. Pull the meat out of the tail and cut it into medallions. Remove the claw meat from their shells and leave them whole.

salad of crab and avocado

THIS SALAD is substantial enough to serve as a summertime entrée when accompanied by cornbread to accent the salad's Southwestern flavor profile. Serve the salad in large martini or margarita glasses for a dramatic presentation.

MAKES 8 SERVINGS

FRESH TOMATO SALSA

½ cup small-dice red pepper

2 plum tomatoes, cored and chopped

2 scallions, thinly sliced on the diagonal

1 garlic clove, minced

2 tbsp chopped cilantro

2 tsp minced jalapeño

3 tbsp lime juice, or as needed

Salt as needed

Freshly ground black pepper as needed

2 ripe avocados, cut into small dice

2½ cups lump crabmeat, picked

¼ cup sour cream

1. To make the salsa: Toss together the red pepper, tomatoes, scallions, garlic, cilantro, and jalapeño. Season to taste with lime juice, salt, and black pepper. Set aside to rest at room temperature for about 20 minutes.

2. Toss together the avocados with 1 tablespoon lime juice. Season to taste with additional lime juice, salt, and pepper. Set aside.

3. To assemble the salad, layer the avocado mixture, followed by the crab, and top with the salsa and sour cream.

potato salad with tuna, olives, and red peppers

Rin Ran

THIS SALAD is best if the potatoes are warm when you dress and toss the salad. We recommend that you search out good quality oil-packed tuna for this recipe. Specialty shops and delicatessens are a good source. Water-packed tuna, especially albacore, is fine, but the salad won't be quite as luscious.

MAKES 4 SERVINGS

1 lb new potatoes

Salt as needed

2 large red bell peppers, seeded and diced

1 cup pitted green olives

One 8-oz can oil-packed tuna, drained

6 tbsp extra-virgin olive oil

2 tbsp red wine vinegar

1 tsp ground cumin

1 tsp mild paprika

Freshly ground black pepper as needed

¼ cup coarsely chopped flat leaf parsley

1. Cook the potatoes in lightly salted water until they are just done, tender but firm enough to slice, 20 to 25 minutes. Let cool slightly, then peel and dice.

2. Combine the warm diced potatoes, diced peppers, and olives in a salad bowl. Break the tuna up with your fingertips as you add it to the salad. Set aside.

3. Combine the oil, vinegar, cumin, paprika, black pepper, and salt in a small bowl, whisking until the dressing is combined and thickened. Pour this over the salad ingredients and toss gently until all the ingredients are evenly dressed. Serve on a chilled platter or plates garnished with parsley.

niçoise-style tuna

THIS SALAD gained its name from the town where it is said to have been born, Nice, France. Most traditional recipes call for boiled potatoes and good quality canned tuna, but we enjoy this version with roasted potatoes and broiled tuna. Add herbs like oregano, rosemary, or tarragon to the potatoes before you roast them if you wish.

MAKES 4 SERVINGS

8 new red potatoes, halved or quartered

3 tbsp olive oil

Salt as needed

Freshly ground black pepper as needed

BALSAMIC VINAIGRETTE

3 tbsp balsamic vinegar

½ tsp Dijon-style mustard

⅓ cup extra-virgin olive oil

4 cups mixed salad greens

1 cup haricots verts, steamed and chilled

1 cup cherry tomatoes, halved if desired

16 Niçoise olives

4 hard-cooked eggs, cut into eighths

½ lb tuna fillet, trimmed and cut into 4 portions

1. Preheat the oven to 350 degrees F.

2. Coat the potatoes with the olive oil and season with salt and pepper. Roast the potatoes in a 350 degrees F oven until tender, 30 to 35 minutes.

3. Combine the balsamic vinegar, mustard, a pinch of salt, and pepper and blend well. Add ⅓ cup olive oil while whisking until the dressing is thickened. Add the salad greens and haricots verts and toss until evenly coated. Using tongs, lift the greens and beans letting the dressing drain back into the bowl. Place on chilled plates or a platter. Arrange the tomatoes, olives, and hard-cooked eggs on the greens.

4. Preheat the broiler on high and position a broiling rack about 2 inches from the heat. Season the tuna with the salt and pepper. Broil the tuna until it is cooked to the desired doneness, about 3 minutes on each side for medium-rare. Slice the tuna and fan it on top of the greens along with the potatoes. Spoon the dressing that remains in the salad bowl over the top of the salad and serve at once.

cobb salad

COBB SALAD was created at the Brown Derby Restaurant in Hollywood, California. Various interpretations may call for either chicken or turkey. The garnish suggestions here are typical, but some versions have included watercress, celery, Cheddar cheese, hard-boiled eggs, black olives, or alfalfa sprouts.

MAKES 8 SERVINGS

2 lb chicken breasts, boneless and skinless

2 tsp salt, or to taste

1 tsp freshly ground black pepper, or to taste

1 tbsp vegetable oil

16 bacon slices

8 cups torn romaine lettuce, washed and dried

½ cup Cobb Salad Vinaigrette (recipe follows)

1½ cups diced plum tomatoes

2 cups crumbled blue cheese

2 ripe Haas avocados, sliced ¼ inch thick

½ cup thinly sliced scallions, cut on diagonal

8 hard-cooked eggs, quartered

1. Preheat the oven to 400 degrees F.

2. Season the chicken breasts with salt and pepper. Heat the vegetable oil in a large sauté pan over medium-high heat until it shimmers. Add the chicken and sauté until golden brown on both sides, 2 to 3 minutes on each side. Place the pan in the preheated oven and cook the chicken to an internal temperature of 165 degrees F. Cool and cut into ¼-inch-thick slices on the diagonal.

3. Sauté the bacon until crisp. Drain on absorbent paper and crumble into small pieces.

4. Toss the romaine with the vinaigrette and make a bed on chilled plates or a chilled platter. Top with chicken slices, diced tomatoes, blue cheese, avocado, scallions, hard-cooked eggs, and crumbled bacon. Serve at once.

Cobb Salad Vinaigrette

MAKES 2 CUPS

¼ cup water

6 tbsp red wine vinegar

½ tsp sugar

2½ tsp lemon juice

1¼ tsp salt, or to taste

½ tsp freshly ground black pepper, or to taste

½ tsp coarse grain mustard

2 garlic cloves, minced

1¼ cup extra-virgin olive oil

1. Blend together all of the ingredients except for the olive oil. Allow the flavors to marry for 5 minutes.

2. Add the olive oil and whisk thoroughly. It may be necessary to blend the dressing together again before serving.

minty thai-style chicken salad

THE QUANTITY of mint in this salad is significant. Throughout Southeast Asia herbs often are included as a major ingredient, rather than being relegated into a supporting role as a garnish or decoration.

MAKES 4 TO 6 SERVINGS

1 tbsp canola oil

1 tbsp dried red pepper flakes

½ tsp mild or hot paprika

⅔ lb minced chicken breast or thigh meat

3 tbsp fish sauce

2 tsp brown sugar

2 beefsteak tomatoes, seeded and chopped

¼ cup minced scallion

⅓ cup lime juice

½ cup mint leaves, torn

1 tbsp minced lemongrass

3 wild lime leaves, cut into fine slivers

4 to 6 red-leaf lettuce leaves

½ head Napa cabbage, cored and cut into 2-inch-wide wedges

12 cilantro sprigs

1. Heat the oil in a sauté pan over low heat. Add the red pepper flakes and paprika and sauté, stirring constantly, until aromatic, about 10 seconds. Add the chicken, fish sauce, and brown sugar and increase the heat to medium. Sauté, stirring frequently, until chicken is no longer pink, 4 to 5 minutes.

2. Transfer the chicken to a bowl and add the tomatoes, scallion, lime juice, mint leaves, lemongrass, and lime leaves. Toss the salad until all ingredients are evenly coated.

3. Serve the salad on lettuce leaves accompanied with a wedge of cabbage. Drizzle some of the juices from the bottom of the salad bowl over each serving. Garnish with cilantro.

hue chicken salad

Ga Bop

YOU CAN use either poached or roasted chicken to make this salad. If you can't find *rau ram* (see page 168), substitute an equal quantity of basil and mint. Vietnamese *sambal* is a fiery hot chile paste. You can substitute a good hot sauce if it cannot be found.

MAKES 4 SERVINGS

½ medium onion, sliced thin

1½ lb shredded cooked chicken meat

¼ cup rau ram leaves, torn

¼ cup mint leaves, torn

¼ cup minced cilantro leaves and stems

2 Thai bird chiles, thinly sliced

2 tbsp lime juice

1 tbsp peanut oil

1 tbsp fish sauce

1 tbsp Vietnamese sambal

2 tsp sugar or as needed

Salt as needed

Freshly ground black pepper as needed

4 banana leaves, cut into large triangles

4 Boston lettuce leaves

2 cups steamed jasmine rice (see page 160)

½ cup crispy fried shallots (page 11)

1 red Fresno chile, sliced paper thin

1. Combine the onion slices with enough cold water to cover and refrigerate for at least 30 minutes and up to 2 hours.

2. Combine the chicken, rau ram, mint, cilantro, and Thai bird chiles in a large bowl. Drain the onion slices and add them to the chicken. Add the lime juice, peanut oil, fish sauce, and sambal to the salad and toss gently until combined. Season to taste with sugar, salt, and pepper.

3. Arrange the banana leaves and Boston lettuce on chilled plates. Top with the salad and serve with steamed rice, crispy shallots, and the Fresno chile.

neopolitan-style pizza

with Mozzarella, Prosciutto, and Roasted Red Pepper

FRESH MOZZARELLA and a drizzle of fruity, extra-virgin olive oil give this pizza a special character.

MAKES 4 SERVINGS

2 red bell peppers

Two 12-inch Pizza Crusts (recipe follows)

½ cup Tomato Sauce (page 165)

¾ lb sliced fresh mozzarella

8 thin slices prosciutto

Extra-virgin olive oil as needed

Salt as needed

Freshly ground black pepper as needed

1. Preheat the oven to 450 degrees F. Prepare baking sheets by scattering them with cornmeal.

2. Char the red peppers directly in a gas flame until they are charred and blistered on all sides. Immediately place in a bowl or plastic bag and cover the peppers. Once they are cool enough to handle, pull away the skin and cut out the stem, ribs, and seeds. Cut into strips. Set aside.

3. Shape the pizza dough into two 12-inch rounds. Transfer the dough rounds to the cornmeal-scattered baking sheets. Bake the crust until firmed and set, about 10 minutes.

4. Spread ¼ cup tomato sauce on each pizza. Layer the cheese, prosciutto, and peppers on the pizza crusts. Drizzle with a little olive oil and season with salt and pepper.

5. Bake the pizza until the crust is golden brown and crisp, 12 to 14 minutes. Let the pizza rest for 5 minutes before serving.

Pizza Crust

MAKES ONE 16-INCH OR TWO 12-INCH PIZZAS

3½ cups bread flour, plus as needed

½ cup semolina or durum flour

1½ tsp active dry yeast

1½ cups room-temperature water (68–76°F)

3 tbsp olive oil, plus as needed

2 tsp salt

Cornmeal for dusting

1. To prepare the dough, combine the flours and yeast in the bowl of a stand mixer fitted with the dough hook. Add the water, olive oil, and salt and mix on low speed for 2 minutes.

2. Increase the speed to medium and knead until the dough is quite elastic but still a little sticky, 4 minutes.

3. Transfer the dough to a lightly oiled bowl, turn the dough to coat it with the oil, cover with plastic wrap or a damp towel, and allow to rise in a warm place until nearly doubled in size, about 30 minutes.

4. Fold the dough gently, cover, and let rest until relaxed, 15–20 minutes, before cutting it into 2 equal pieces, if necessary, and rounding the dough into a smooth ball(s).

5. Cover the dough and let rest another 15–20 minutes before shaping into a pizza crust.

CLOCKWISE FROM UPPER LEFT *When preparing fresh mozzarella, work the curds gently so that your finished product is smooth, but not tough. When shaping prepared mozzarella, it is easy, but not essential, to work in ice water, as the cheese will set as it cools; the finished cheese, however, should always be stored in water until ready to be used. Immediately after roasting peppers, place them in a bowl covered with plastic wrap and let them steam for a few minutes; this will make it easier to remove the charred skin. The finished pizza should rest 5 minutes before cutting and serving.*

barbecued chicken pizza

with Fresh Tomato Salsa

WE'VE GIVEN the instructions to make the barbecued pizza here, but if you have grilled or barbecued chicken, turkey, or other meats, use them instead. This is a perfect way to use up the last bit of a Sunday afternoon cook-out.

MAKES 8 SERVINGS

BARBECUE SAUCE

2 tsp butter

¾ cup chopped onion

2 tsp minced garlic

½ cup tomato paste

¼ cup brewed coffee

1 canned chipotle pepper, packed in adobo

3 tbsp apple cider vinegar

3 tbsp apple cider

3 tbsp brown sugar

1½ tbsp Worcestershire sauce

8 oz chicken breasts, boneless, trimmed

One 16-inch Pizza Crust (page 188)

1 cup thinly sliced Monterey Jack cheese

1 cup Fresh Tomato Salsa (page 179)

2 tbsp minced scallions

1. Preheat a gas grill to medium-high; leave one burner off. If you are using a charcoal grill, build a fire and let it burn down until the coals are glowing red with a moderate coating of white ash. Spread the coals in an even bed on one side of the grill. Clean the cooking grate.

2. To prepare the barbecue sauce: Heat the butter in a saucepan over low heat. Add the onion and garlic and sauté, stirring frequently, until they are translucent, about 5 minutes. Add the tomato paste, coffee, chipotle, apple cider vinegar, apple cider, sugar, and Worcestershire sauce. Simmer the sauce over low heat until it has thickened slightly, about 15 minutes.

3. Grill the chicken over direct heat until marked on all sides, about 1 minute per side. Finish cooking the chicken over indirect heat, covered, turning as necessary and brushing with the barbecue sauce, until cooked through and the juices run clear, 10 to 12 minutes. When the chicken is cool enough to handle, slice it thinly. (You also may barbecue the chicken up to 2 days in advance. Keep it wrapped and refrigerated until you are ready to make the pizzas.)

4. Preheat the oven to 450°F. Prepare a baking sheet by scattering it with cornmeal. Shape the pizza dough into a 16-inch round. Transfer the dough round to the cornmeal-scattered baking sheet, and bake the crust until it is firmed and set, about 10 minutes.

5. Arrange the cheese around the outer edge of the disk. Arrange the sliced chicken on top of the cheese. Place salsa in the middle of the pizza. Bake the pizza in the oven until the crust is golden brown and crisp, 12 to 14 minutes. Garnish with the scallions Let the pizza rest for 5 minutes before cutting and serving.

spinach and jack cheese quesadillas

You don't have to use all three types of Monterey Jack called for in this recipe, but adding a touch of aged jack cheese as well as hot pepper cheese gives this dish an extra level of flavor.

MAKES 4 SERVINGS

3 tbsp olive oil

12 cups (lightly packed) spinach leaves

1 tsp salt

½ tsp ground black pepper

8 large flour tortillas

2 cups grated Monterey Jack cheese

½ cup Pepper Jack cheese

2 cups grated aged Jack cheese

1. Heat the olive oil in large skillet over medium heat. Add the spinach, season with salt and black pepper, and cook, stirring frequently, until tender, about 10 minutes. Remove and drain the spinach.

2. Heat a large cast iron or nonstick griddle or skillet over medium heat until very hot. Working with one tortilla at a time, place the tortilla in the griddle or skillet. Top with the cheeses and spinach and put a second tortilla on top. Grill on the first side until crisp and golden, 3 to 4 minutes, turn, and cook on the second side. Cut into wedges and serve immediately.

whole-wheat quesadillas
with Chicken, Jalapeño Jack, and Mango Salsa

LOOK FOR whole-wheat flour tortillas in the refrigerated section of your supermarket. Serve these healthy quesadillas with a black bean salad to make a satisfying meal.

MAKES 4 SERVINGS

1 tbsp vegetable oil

1½ lb chicken breasts, boneless, skinless

Salt as needed

Freshly ground black pepper as needed

1½ cup diced mango

½ cup diced papaya

1 tsp minced canned chipotle pepper

2 tbsp orange juice

2 tbsp lime juice

1½ cups grated Jalapeño Jack cheese

1 cup thinly sliced scallions

½ cup rough-chopped peanuts, toasted

8 large whole-wheat flour tortillas

2 tbsp peanut oil

1. Preheat the oven to 400 degrees F.

2. Heat the vegetable oil over high heat in a large sauté pan. Season the chicken with the salt and pepper. Cook the chicken breasts until golden brown on all sides, 8 to 10 minutes. Place the chicken in the oven until cooked through, 10 to 12 minutes total. Allow the chicken to cool until it can be handled easily and then shred the chicken into small pieces.

3. To make mango salsa: Combine the mango, papaya, chipotle pepper, orange juice, and lime juice in a small bowl. Set aside. If the salsa is made in advance, keep it refrigerated unit you are ready to serve it.

4. To assemble the quesadillas: Divide the chicken, cheese, scallions, and peanuts evenly among 4 tortillas. Top each quesadilla with second tortilla.

5. Heat a little peanut oil in a large sauté pan over high heat until it shimmers. Place a quesadilla in the pan and sauté until brown and crisp on the first side, about 3 minutes. Turn once and brown the quesadilla on the second side, another 2 minutes. Repeat with remaining quesadillas, adding more peanut oil as necessary.

6. Cut each quesadilla into quarters and serve with the mango salsa.

grilled chicken sandwich

with Pancetta, Arugula, and Aïoli

a FEW SIMPLE components, properly paired, can produce outstanding results. This flavorful grilled sandwich has an elegant twist with garlicky mayonnaise and the light peppery flavor of arugula. To keep the pancetta from causing fare-ups on the grill, cook it separately in a skillet over medium heat.

MAKES 4 SERVINGS

½ cup mayonnaise

1 garlic clove, minced

4 boneless, skinless chicken breasts, about 1½ lb total

Salt as needed

Freshly ground black pepper as needed

3 tbsp olive oil, or as needed

8 slices sourdough bread

½ bunch arugula, trimmed, washed, and dried

8 slices pancetta, cooked until crisp

1. Combine the mayonnaise and garlic to make the aïoli. Set aside.

2. Preheat a gas grill to medium-high. If you are using a charcoal grill, build a fire and let it burn down until the coals are glowing red with a moderate coating of white ash. Spread the coals in an even bed. Clean the cooking grate.

3. Pound the chicken breasts to an even thickness. Season generously with salt and pepper and brush with 1 tablespoon olive oil. Grill the chicken over direct heat until marked on all sides, about 3 minutes per side. Finish cooking the chicken over indirect heat, covered, turning as necessary, until cooked through and the juices run clear, 10 to 12 minutes.

4. Lightly brush the slices of bread with the remaining olive oil. Grill the bread, turning as necessary, until it is marked and crispy on both sides, about 2 minutes.

5. Spread 1 tablespoon of the aïoli on one side of each slice of grilled bread. To assemble each sandwich, place a few leaves of arugula, 2 slices of crispy pancetta, and the chicken breast on one slice of bread; top with a second slice. Slice each sandwich diagonally and serve at once.

grilled focaccia sandwich

with Bacon and Avocado

i F YOU want to make your own focaccia, use the recipe for pizza crust (page 188). Instead of shaping it into a pizza crust, shape the dough into round that will fit in an 8- or 9-inch round baking pan. Dimple the top of the dough after it has nearly doubled in size, drizzle generously with olive oil, and add any other toppings you wish, such as sautéed onions, roasted garlic, or minced herbs. Bake at 375 degrees F until the crust is golden brown, about 20 minutes.

MAKES 6 SERVINGS

¼ cup extra-virgin olive oil, or as needed

1 tbsp balsamic vinegar

3 beefsteak tomatoes, sliced thin

2 ripe Haas avocados, sliced

1 tsp lemon juice

1 tbsp minced garlic

1 tsp salt

¼ tsp ground black pepper

6 onion or plain focaccia squares or two 8-inch round focaccia

¼ to ½ cup mayonnaise

6 lettuce leaves, rinsed and dried

12 slices cooked bacon

1. Combine 2 tablespoons olive oil and the vinegar. Add the sliced tomatoes and toss gently to coat them. Set aside.

2. Slice the avocados and sprinkle with the lemon juice to keep them from turning brown. Set aside.

3. Heat a griddle or cast iron skillet over medium heat or preheat the broiler to high. In a small bowl, combine the remaining olive oil with the garlic. Season with salt and pepper. Set aside.

4. Cut the focaccia in half horizontally and brush with the garlic oil mixture. Griddle or broil, oiled sided facing down, until toasted, about 4 minutes

5. Spread the mayonnaise on the toasted focaccia and then layer the sandwich filling on top of the bread: lettuce leaves, sliced tomatoes, bacon, and finally, sliced avocado. Close the sandwich and serve at once.

ham, brie, and tomato sandwich

on Sourdough Bread

CHOOSING RIPE brie can be a challenge. If possible, press the cheese with your fingertip right through any wrappings around the cheese. It should yield to light pressure if it is properly ripened. Brie has the best flavor and texture when it is served at room temperature, not straight from the refrigerator.

MAKES 6 SERVINGS

12 slices sourdough bread or 2 sourdough baguettes

3 tbsp whole-grain mustard, or as needed

1¼ lb thinly sliced ham

1 lb brie cheese, sliced ¼-inch thick,
     rind removed

2 beefsteak tomatoes, sliced thin

Salt as needed

Freshly ground black pepper as needed

Spread the sliced bread with mustard. If you are using baguettes, cut them in half horizontally and spread with mustard. Add the ham and brie. Top with the sliced tomatoes and season to taste with salt and pepper. Add a second slice of bread, slice on the diagonal and serve.

A FRENCH HAM SANDWICH

Sandwiches made on crusty rolls filled with sliced ham are very popular throughout France. In this county, we tend to use a boiled (or cooked) ham for sandwiches. If you can find the famous Jambon de Bayonne produced in France, you'll have found a wonderful cured raw ham, much like Prosciutto and Smithfield hams. A red seal on the ham is a guarantee that the raw ham has been massaged with a mixture of salt from Salies-de-Béarn, saltpeter, sugar, pepper, and herbs. Jambon de Bayonne is air-cured for at least 130 days before it is ready to sell.

oyster po' boy with rémoulade

T HERE ARE several explanations about its origin, but one popular theory reports that the po' boy sandwich—a true New Orleans specialty—was invented in 1920 by Benny and Clovis Martin at Martin Brother's Grocery where it was offered to streetcar workers then on strike. In this version, oysters are rolled in fresh bread crumbs, sautéed, and served in French rolls with a classic rémoulade sauce.

MAKES 8 SERVINGS

½ cup mayonnaise

2 scallions, minced

¼ cup minced celery

2 tbsp minced parsley

2 tbsp dill pickle relish

2 tbsp red wine vinegar

4 tsp Dijon mustard

4 tsp minced capers, drained

2 tsp Worcestershire sauce

4 dashes hot pepper sauce, optional

1½ cups bread crumbs

¾ cup all-purpose flour

1 tsp freshly ground black pepper, or to taste

½ tsp cayenne pepper

4 dozen oysters, shucked

4 large eggs, beaten

½ cup canola oil, or as needed

8 crusty French rolls, cut in half

2 beefsteak tomatoes, thinly sliced

1 cup shredded romaine lettuce

2 lemons, cut into wedges

1. To prepare the rémoulade: Combine the mayonnaise, scallions, celery, parsley, relish, vinegar, mustard, capers, Worcestershire sauce, and pepper sauce, if using, in a bowl. Set aside.

2. Combine the bread crumbs, flour, black pepper, and cayenne. Toss with your fingertips to combine. Drain the oysters of any liquid and dry thoroughly. Dip the oysters, one at a time, into the beaten egg and roll in the bread crumb mixture. Heat ¼ cup of the oil in a large skillet until it shimmers. Add half of the oysters and fry, turning once, until the oysters are browned and cooked through, 4 to 5 minutes. Repeat with the remaining oil and oysters.

3. Toast the roll halves. Layer the oysters, tomato slices, and lettuce evenly on 8 halves and top with the remaining halves. Serve with the rémoulade and lemon wedges.

crabmeat and shrimp sandwich

*i*T'S EASY to find shrimp and crabmeat of excellent quality that is already cooked and prepared for delicious sandwiches. Check with your local fish market or favorite supermarket for the days these prepared items are freshest.

MAKES 8 SERVINGS

½ lb crabmeat, cooked, picked over for shells

½ lb shrimp, cooked, peeled, diced

½ cup mayonnaise

¼ cup sour cream

1 tbsp white wine vinegar

1 garlic clove, minced

2 tsp Dijon mustard

2 tsp curry powder

¼ tsp salt, or to taste

¼ tsp freshly ground black pepper, or to taste

8 pitas

1 beefsteak tomato, thinly sliced

1 red onion, thinly sliced

1 avocado, thinly sliced, optional

1 container alfalfa sprouts

1. Place the picked crabmeat and diced shrimp in a bowl and set aside.

2. In a small bowl, stir together the mayonnaise, sour cream, vinegar, garlic, mustard, curry powder, salt, and pepper. Stir the mayonnaise mixture into the crabmeat and shrimp until combined. Split open the pitas and line each with the tomato, onion, and avocado, if using. Divide the crabmeat mixture evenly between the pitas and tuck some of the alfalfa sprouts into each.

gyro with tzatziki sauce

gYRO MEAT is infused with the traditional Greek flavors of marjoram and rosemary. The meat in this sandwich will have a slightly crumblier texture than the gyro meat found in most Greek restaurants, but with a superior flavor.

MAKES 6 SERVINGS

GYRO MEAT

1 lb ground lamb

1 lb ground beef

1 cup finely minced onion, squeezed

1 tbsp finely minced garlic

1 tbsp dried marjoram

1 tbsp dried rosemary

2 tsp salt

½ tsp freshly ground black pepper

6 pitas

3 cups shredded romaine lettuce

2 plum tomatoes, seeded and cut into medium dice

⅓ cup medium-dice sweet onion

1½ cups Tzatziki Sauce (recipe follows)

1. Combine the lamb, beef, onion, garlic, marjoram, rosemary, salt, and pepper and stir until the meats and seasonings are evenly blended. Cover and refrigerate until very cold, at least 2 hours. Chill the bowl and blade of a food processor in the freezer at the same time you are chilling the meat.

2. Preheat the oven to 350°F and lightly oil a baking pan. (If you prefer, you can prepare the gyro meat on a rotisserie. Preheat the grill to medium-high and assemble the rotisserie.)

3. Transfer the meat mixture to the chilled food processor bowl and process until a sticky paste forms, about 2 minutes. Spoon the mixture into the prepared baking pan, shaping it with dampened hands into a loaf about 1½ inches thick and 8 inches long. It should not touch the sides of the pan. (If pre-paring the meat on a rotisserie, pack it around the round in a cylinder.) Cook the meat until it is completely cooked through (an internal temperature of 150°F), about 35 to 40 minutes.

4. Cool the meat to room temperature, remove from the loaf pan, and wrap well. Chill the meat in the refrigerator for at least 8 and up to 12 hours prior to slicing thinly.

5. Heat a griddle or skillet over medium-high heat. Add the pitas one at a time and griddle until toasted and very pliable; set aside. Add the sliced gyro meat to the griddle and cook until hot and lightly colored, about 2 minutes. Fill each pita with the sliced gyro meat and top with lettuce, tomatoes, and onion. Wrap the sandwich in paper and use a toothpick to hold the sandwich closed. Serve with the tzatziki sauce.

Tzatziki Sauce

MAKES 1½ CUPS

½ cup plain yogurt

½ cup sour cream

½ cup grated cucumber, squeezed dry

1 tsp minced garlic

1 tbsp extra-virgin olive oil

1 tbsp minced fresh dill

1 tsp lemon juice or as needed

½ tsp grated lemon zest

Salt as needed

Freshly ground black pepper as needed

Combine the yogurt, sour cream, cucumber, and garlic in a food processor and puree until smooth. Transfer to a bowl and fold in the olive oil, dill, lemon juice, and zest. Stir until combined and season to taste with salt and pepper. Keep refrigerated until ready to serve.

saigon subs

Bahn Mi

bAHN MI are delectable sub sandwiches popular in Vietnam and a reminder of the strong influence the French have had on Vietnamese cuisine. The quintessential Vietnamese flavorings include lemongrass, galangal, and fish sauce, as well as a fresh "salad" of green papaya, coconut, and jalapeño.

MAKES 6 SERVINGS

¼ cup diced green papaya

¼ cup grated fresh coconut

2 tbsp chopped pan-roasted peanuts (page 44)

1 tbsp minced jalapeño

3 tbsp chopped cilantro leaves

2 tbsp minced scallion

1 tbsp jaggery

1 tbsp lime juice or as needed

1 tsp hot sauce or as needed

2 baguettes

3 tbsp melted butter, melted

1 lb Viet Cinnamon Pâté (recipe follows), sliced thin

1. Combine the papaya, coconut, peanuts, jalapeño, cilantro, scallion, and jaggery in a small bowl. Add lime juice and hot sauce to taste. Cover and refrigerate until you are ready to assemble the subs.

2. Preheat a skillet or griddle over medium-high heat. Cut the baguettes in half, then slice them open horizontally. Brush the insides with the melted butter. Toast the baguettes on the griddle, buttered side down, until golden brown, about 2 minutes. Remove from the griddle and set aside.

3. Add the slices of paté to the griddle and cook until hot and lightly colored on both sides, about 2 minutes. Fill the toasted baguettes with the pâté slices and then top with the papaya-coconut salad. Serve at once with additional hot sauce.

Viet Cinnamon Pâté

MAKES 1 POUND

2 tbsp wheat or rice starch

3 tbsp fish sauce

2 tbsp soy sauce

¼ cup minced lemongrass

One 2-inch piece galangal, minced

2 tsp sugar

1 tsp freshly ground black pepper

½ tsp ground cinnamon

1 lb boneless pork shoulder, untrimmed

½ cup ice-cold water

1. To make the spice paste: Combine the wheat or rice starch, fish sauce, soy sauce, lemongrass, galangal, sugar, pepper, and cinnamon in a large bowl. Stir well and add cold water a teaspoon at a time to make a loose paste.

2. Cut the pork into ¼-inch cubes and add to the spice paste. Turn to coat the pork evenly, cover, and refrigerate until very cold, at least 2 hours. Spread the meat in an even layer on a baking sheet and place in the freezer for 15 to 20 minutes. Chill the bowl and blade of a food processor and a mixing bowl in the freezer at the same time that you are chilling the pork.

3. Preheat the oven to 350°F and bring a large kettle of water to a boil for a water bath. Brush an 8-inch loaf pan with oil.

4. Assemble the food processor. Transfer the semi-frozen pork to the food processor and process until a coarse paste forms, about 1 minute. Transfer ground meat mixture to the chilled mixing bowl and add the ice water (no ice cubes). *(recipe continues on page 206)*

(continued from page 204) Mix the ice water into the pork by hand with a wooden spoon until the water is blended into the paste and the mixture is slightly sticky, about 30 seconds.

5. Spoon the mixture into the prepared loaf pan, packing it into the pan to remove any pockets of air. Smooth the top of the pâté, place the loaf pan in a deep baking dish, and place in the oven. Pour boiling water into the deep baking dish to a depth of 2 inches. Bake the pâté until it is completely cooked (an internal temperature of 150°F), about 35 to 40 minutes.

6. Cool the pâté to room temperature, remove from the loaf pan, and wrap well. Chill the pâté for at least 8 and up to 12 hours before serving.

tempeh club sandwich

TEMPEH IS a soybean cake made from fermenting cooked soybeans and usually includes a rice or grain. It has a firm texture and a nutty flavor that will surprise you if you've never tried it before.

MAKES 4 SERVINGS

1 package tempeh

2 tbsp peanut or canola oil, plus as needed

Salt as needed

Freshly ground black pepper as needed

12 slices whole-grain bread, toasted

½ cup mayonnaise

1 avocado, thinly sliced

¼ cup minced sun dried tomatoes

1 cups sunflower or alfalfa sprouts

1. Slice the tempeh in half lengthwise so that it is half its original thickness. Cut each of those pieces in half again, making 2 smaller rectangles. There should be 8 pieces of tempeh (4 from each original piece), each piece approximately the size of a slice of bread.

2. Heat a sauté pan over medium-high heat. Add 2 tablespoons oil to the hot pan, then add half of the tempeh to the pan and sauté until golden on the first side. Turn and continue to cook until golden on the second side. Remove the tempeh from the pan, season with salt and pepper, and reserve. Repeat with the remaining tempeh, adding more oil to the pan as needed.

3. To assemble the sandwiches, spread the slices of toasted bread with the mayonnaise. Top 4 of the toasted slices with the tempeh. Top the tempeh with a second slice of toasted bread and then add the avocado slices, the sun dried tomatoes, the sprouts, and a third piece of toasted bread.

4. Use large sandwich picks to hold the sandwiches together if desired and cut each sandwich in half or into quarters. Serve the sandwiches at once.

madeira-glazed portobello sandwiches

*P*ORTOBELLO MUSHROOMS are actually mature cremini mushrooms and have a dense, meaty texture when cooked. They easily can be prepared for this recipe a day ahead. Cool the broiled mushroom caps completely and refrigerate until needed. Slice the mushrooms and allow them to return to room temperature prior to assembling the sandwiches.

MAKES 8 SERVINGS

8 portobello mushrooms

¼ cup Madeira

3 tbsp olive oil

2 garlic cloves, bruised

½ tsp dried oregano

2 tsp salt, or to taste

1 tsp freshly ground black pepper, or to taste

3 cups sliced onion

8 hard rolls, split

8 thin slices Swiss cheese

4 cups mixed baby greens

1. Preheat the broiler and place the oven rack in the upper third of the oven.

2. Remove the stems from the mushrooms, use a sharp paring knife to cut away the gills, and discard. Combine the Madeira, 2 tablespoons of the olive oil, garlic cloves, oregano, 1 teaspoon of salt, and ½ teaspoon of the pepper in a large bowl. Add the mushrooms and toss to coat. Set aside for 10 minutes to marinate.

3. Heat the remaining tablespoon of olive oil in a sauté pan set over medium-high heat. Add the onion and sauté until soft and translucent, 5 to 6 minutes. Season with the remaining 1 teaspoon of salt and ½ teaspoon of pepper.

4. Place the mushrooms on a baking sheet, brush with the marinade, and broil until browned and tender, about 4 minutes on each side. When cool enough to handle, thinly slice each mushroom and place one entire sliced mushroom on the bottom half of each roll. Top with 1 slice of cheese.

5. Place the bottom half of each roll with the mushroom and cheese on a baking pan and broil until the cheese is melted, about 2 minutes.

6. Top each sandwich with ¼ cup of the onions, ½ cup of the greens, and the top half of the roll.

index

WEIGHT MEASURES CONVERSION

U.S. and Metric. Values have been rounded.

¼ ounce	8 grams
½ ounce	15 grams
1 ounce	30 grams
4 ounces	115 grams
8 ounces (½ pound)	225 grams
16 ounces (1 pound)	450 grams
32 ounces (2 pounds)	900 grams
40 ounces (2¼ pounds)	1 kilogram

VOLUME MEASURES CONVERSION

U.S. and Metric. Values have been rounded.

1 teaspoon	5 milliliters
1 tablespoon	15 milliliters
1 fluid ounce (2 tablespoons)	30 milliliters
2 fluid ounces (¼ cup)	60 milliliters
8 fluid ounces (1 cup)	240 milliliters
16 fluid ounces (1 pint)	480 milliliters
32 fluid ounces (1 quart)	950 milliliters
128 fluid ounces (1 gallon)	3.75 liters

TEMPERATURE CONVERSION

Degrees Farenheit and Celcius. Values have been rounded.

32°F	0°C
40°F	4°C
140°F	60°C
150°F	65°C
160°F	70°C
170°F	75°C
212°F	100°C
275°F	135°C
300°F	150°C
325°F	165°C
350°F	175°C
375°F	190°C
400°F	205°C
425°F	220°C
450°F	230°C
475°F	245°C
500°F	260°C

A Note on the Type

American type designer Carol Twombly's 1989 digital revival for
the Adobe Corporation of the typefaces of the esteemed English typecutter,
William Caslon, is notable for its faithful reproduction of both the aesthetic details and
historical spirit of Caslon's work. The version used here, which features Adobe's OpenType
technology and an extensive multilingual character set, represents both a technologically
advanced and historically faithful reproduction of Caslon's types, the pinnacle of
English Baroque type design and a stalwart of printing and publishing
since their introduction in the mid-eighteenth century.

Art direction, design, and composition by Kevin Hanek

Printed in Singapore by Imago